Multi-faceted Approaches to Challenges and Coping in Law Enforcement

Konstantinos Papazoglou • Katy Kamkar
Editors

Multi-faceted Approaches to Challenges and Coping in Law Enforcement

Police Badge Is One Badge

Springer

Editors
Konstantinos Papazoglou
ProWellness Inc.
Woodbridge, ON, Canada

Katy Kamkar
Toronto, ON, Canada

ISBN 978-3-031-62824-5 ISBN 978-3-031-62825-2 (eBook)
https://doi.org/10.1007/978-3-031-62825-2

This Springer imprint is published by the registered company Springer Nature Switzerland AG
The registered company address is: Gewerbestrasse 11, 6330 Cham, Switzerland

Foreword

Until relatively recently, the significance of mental health factors in society generally has attracted less attention than reality demanded. This resulted in less than adequate care for many who needed treatment and support, increased costs to society, ineffective policies and harmful effects and limitations on mental health services.

These mental health factors also impact policing and law enforcement globally. They comprise increasing challenges and demands for attention from police officers as they carry out regular patrol services. Police officers do not expect, nor are they adequately prepared, to recognize mental health issues and respond in the best interests of individuals and society. The underlying message of these trends is the desperate need for politicians, health professionals and police leaders to understand what is happening and rethink community responses. With the benefit of hindsight, an important message is that policing, mental health and public health, more broadly, must work together for the benefit of all involved. Resistance to change, ignorance and hostility within the relevant professions are major obstacles. Many political leaders, especially at local levels, do not want to get involved as many members of the public do not understand the significance of the issues and financial and other resources are very limited.

During the past two decades, however, there have been numerous examples emerging globally that it is necessary, urgent and possible to approach these problems differently.

Focusing on police officers' wellness, health and resilience is a major component of this changing environment and the focus of this book.

A holistic approach is essential if these new approaches are to be successful. Academics, mental health professionals and police leaders must revise recruiting policies, training and professional development programs which emphasize prevention, based on well-informed research. These are key factors in reducing operational stress injuries and trauma to optimize occupational health and safety.

The eight chapters in this book, ranging from lived experiences, better data supporting interventions, a systems approach, a biopsychosocial approach to officer wellness and the importance of strong professional partnerships, provide a comprehensive approach to reaching the desired outcomes.

I commend this timely book to police members at all levels, academics, first responders, politicians and members of the general community.

Richard F. Southby

Dean and Distinguished Professor
of Global Health Emeritus, Milken
Institute School of Public Health
The George Washington University
Washington, DC, USA

Introduction

Multi-faceted Approaches to Challenges and Coping in Law Enforcement: Police Badge Is One Badge delves into the compelling world of law enforcement, exploring the multifarious challenges officers face. This book unveils an array of perspectives, strategies, and coping mechanisms in relation to health and wellness to show the complexities of the police profession. As we journey through the pages of this enlightening work, we discover innovative health and wellness approaches, and unyielding spirit that define those who proudly wear the badge.

Impact of Occupational Stress and Pathways to Improve Mental Health in Public Safety Personnel

Police are exposed to repeated traumatic events, in addition to experiencing occupational stressors, and operational and organizational stressors (Carleton et al., 2019; Oliphant et al., 2016; Komarovskaya et al., 2011). Exposures to potentially traumatic incidents as well as occupational stressors increase the risk for psychological and physical injuries. Findings indicate a positive association between exposure to traumatic events and occupational stressors with mental health conditions (Carleton et al., 2018). Both are found to independently contribute to mental health conditions (Carleton et al., 2020).

Occupational stress at the individual level such as risk of negative physical and mental health conditions and at the organizational level such as absenteeism, reduced productivity, staff turnover and high risk of accidents have shown to be costly (Cooper et al., 1976, 1994). When struggling with work-related strains, there is a greater tendency to use unhealthy coping strategies and a reduced tendency to use healthy adaptive coping strategies (e.g., Meunier et al., 2019), in turn, furthering work strains and exacerbating health conditions and stress levels.

Thus, any organizational health must encompass measures to include prevention and interventions at the system, organizational, and individual levels.

Looking into the public safety personnel occupations, studies (McCreary et al., 2006; Toch et al., 2022) indicate that the occupational stressors related to high work demands, low resources, low control, and low social support, and perception of poor organizational justice can be divided into organizational (e.g., a lack of appropriate resources) and operational (e.g., job-related risk of injury) stressors.

Policymakers need to explore pathways to reduce occupational stressors to support the mental health of public safety personnel such as by building increasingly psychologically safe workplaces (Carleton et al., 2020), including changes to reduce organizational and operational stressors within organizations. Leadership training, leadership support, building on organizational engagement, and improving sleep and social support are among the pathways to help build a stronger and psychologically healthier organization (e.g., Carleton et al., 2020).

Mental Health Conditions and Their Impact

There is a high cost related to mental illness. The cost of mental illnesses is estimated to annually reach US$83 billion (Greenberg et al., 2015) with one of the primary contributing factors of mental illness-related costs being work productivity loss. Absenteeism, presenteeism, and work sick leave are causal factors leading to loss of productivity. In addition to absenteeism, presenteeism is found to be one of the biggest costs to employers. Presenteeism is often thought to present a bigger problem than absenteeism (Boles et al., 2004). Mental health disabilities increase the risk of recurrent mental health disabilities and the risk of non-mental health disabilities in addition to being most costly than physical health disabilities. Findings indicate a return on investment and improved work participation, engagement, and work functioning when the focus is shifted towards the wellness and mental health of the organization and of the worker.

Common mental health conditions such as clinical depression, anxiety disorders, substance use disorders, and post-traumatic stress disorders are increasingly part of mental health education and policies to further mental health promotion, interventions, evidence-based treatment, and return to work disability management.

Anxiety and clinical depression continue to be the leading cause of burden and disease. Depression is the world's leading cause of poor health and disability (World Health Organization, 2017), and found to be the most prevalent single mental disorder (Murray et al., 2013).

Frequently, the presence of depressive symptoms aligns with the clinical identification of major depressive disorder (MDD). This condition is typified by a persistent sad mood and diminished motivation or interest in activities, along with various other manifestations, such as impaired concentration and decision-making, feelings of guilt or worthlessness, disruptions in sleep patterns, irregularities in appetite, fatigue or loss of energy, and thoughts of suicide. Additionally, individuals diagnosed with MDD often encounter difficulties in their social, personal, and occupational functioning (American Psychiatric Association, 2013).

The World Health Organization (World Health Organization, 2017) estimated the prevalence of depression and anxiety in the United States to be 5.9% and 6.3%, respectively. Not only do they contribute to mental health disability leave, but they can also result from disability leaves (Gaspar et al., 2020; Kubo et al., 2014).

The intersection between work leaves and depression and anxiety has also been researched (Gaspar et al., 2020). Depression and anxiety are found to be risk factors for experiencing a future work leave. For individuals without depression or anxiety, work leaves were a risk factor for new-onset depression and anxiety.

The study also found that the probability of individuals having pre-existing and new-onset depression or anxiety varied by the work leave diagnosis. From the research findings, the following health policy implications were recommended (Garpar et al., 2020), including, for instance, the need for targeted screening and treatment of depression and anxiety; mental health treatment needs to take into account the physiological risk factors that contribute to work leaves including diabetes, obesity, and hypertension with appropriate referrals; notifying an employee requiring disability leave that injuries or illnesses warranting time off from work could potentially result in added mental health challenges; the employee has the opportunity to participate in self-evaluating their mental well-being continuously, contributing to the reduction of the stigma around mental health; the screening for depression and anxiety for workers on work leave may be indicated; and the approach of utilizing the work leave diagnosis enables the prioritization of screening of workers more likely to experience anxiety or depression.

Work Disability Interventions and Stigma

Work disability interventions can be cost-effective (Dewa et al., 2021). Dewa et al.'s (2021) systematic literature review focused on economic evaluations of return-to-work interventions aimed at workers with medically certified sickness absences related to mental disorders. Intervention studies were divided into three types: teaching coping skills such as problem-solving for return to work; working with both the worker and supervisor to address barriers to return to work and develop a return-to-work plan; and delivering adequate treatment. The interventions were compared with usual care. Systematic literature review (Dewa et al., 2021) examined the state of knowledge about the cost-effectiveness of return-to-work interventions aimed at workers with medically certified sickness absences related to mental disorders. The authors noted that although the systematic literature review findings reveal that economic evaluations of return-to-work interventions can be cost-effective, the use of economic evaluations for studies of these program types remains in its infancy, and further research is indicated in different disability system contexts.

Stigma plays a role in amplifying the expenses of mental illness. It links to diminished self-esteem, decreased effectiveness, and achievement, and obstructs the willingness to seek assistance when necessary. Stigma contributes disability due to reduced productivity, delay in seeking treatment, and a significant barrier to accessing accommodations at work (e.g., Mojtabai et al., 2011; Clement et al., 2015). Consequently, this could lead to postponing necessary treatment, consequently elevating the possibility of experiencing multiple mental health issues simultaneously, along with an increased risk of both short-term and long-term impact. This highlights the importance of delineating approaches and measures aimed at tackling stigma, as well as methods for diminishing its impact.

Both the perceived relationship with supervisors and feelings of responsibility to organizations are found to be contributors to the decision to disclose (Dewa et al., 2020), findings consistent with those from other countries (e.g., Evans-Lacko et al., 2016).

The relationship with the manager is found as an important factor in the decision (Dewa et al., 2020) in addition to findings suggesting that the relationship could outweigh other occupational stressors such as organizational stressors, recommendations from occupational physicians, or getting workplace accommodations. Manager training to create supportive working relationships with employees is recommended per Dewa et al.'s (2020) study. The following take-home message was provided by Dewa et al. (2020):

Mental health-related workplace stigma can be a barrier to help seeking because it introduces a risk to employment.

Addressing mental health-related stigma in the workplace may be one way to effectively attend to work disability related to mental health issues.

In the disclosure decision, the relationship with the manager plays a central role.

Trainings that teach managers skills to be inclusive and supportive are essential to encouraging disclosure and preventing disability.

Advice from a trusted individual and the experiences of colleagues are also significant factors in the disclosure decision.

Burnout and Its Implications

Burnout is also presently identified as a work-related hazard and found to be associated with a range of adverse outcomes related to health and work ability (e.g., Ahola et al., 2009). Burnout and depression are linked to both financial repercussions and detrimental impacts on the overall well-being of individuals.

Maslach and colleagues (2001) described burnout as a multifaceted condition involving three clusters of symptoms: exhaustion, depersonalization, and reduced sense of personal accomplishment. The exhaustion component of burnout refers to a depletion of emotional and energetic resources. Depersonalization, another aspect of burnout, involves a psychological phenomenon where individuals start to distance themselves emotionally from others, often leading to a sense of cynicism or indifference towards their work or the people they interact with. The reduced sense of personal accomplishment which is the third cluster of symptoms refers to loss of self-efficacy, having feelings of inadequacy or a perceived decline in one's ability to achieve meaningful results or goals. The latter, in turn, can have a devastating impact on one's sense of self, self-esteem, and self-confidence, as well as a profound effect on an individual's well-being and professional life.

It is found to be resulting from cumulative workplace stress where work demands tend to exceed the worker's personal and work resources. Consequently, burnout can result in decreased work productivity and diminished work engagement. This cyclic process can also lead individuals to alter their perceptions, causing them to no longer see their work resources as contributing to personal, psychological, or occupational growth and development.

Burnout can lead to presenteeism, absenteeism, and sick leave. Although not a diagnostic label, burnout can precede or increase the risk of psychological health conditions such as clinical depression, anxiety disorders, substance use disorders, and/or trauma and stressor-related disorders. It is also associated with physical health problems such as diabetes, cardiovascular disease, musculoskeletal pain, and gastrointestinal problems. Burnout is marked by exhaustion, depersonalization/cynicism, and reduced professional efficacy. For instance, exhaustion, whether psychological, emotional, and/or physical, can be marked by depressed mood, low energy, or reduced motivation. There might as well be changes to appetite, sleep, and concentration. The sense of depersonalization and cynicism might consist of emotional numbness, feeling detached from the environment or surroundings. There might be reduced interest in engaging in previously pleasant activities. Reduced professional efficacy is marked by a reduced sense of self-efficacy and no longer trusting self, feeling competent or feeling confident.

Burnout can range from mild fatigue where one might recover quickly after a hard day to extreme and severe levels of fatigue and exhaustion whereby recovery would take longer. Thus, proactive coping interventions at both the individual and organizational levels are essential to reduce the risk of burnout.

Understanding PTSD in Law Enforcement

Police officers encounter a multitude of distressing and traumatic incidents, including, but not limited to, attending scenes of fatal accidents, managing hostage or shooting scenarios, engaging in search and rescue missions, dealing with violence during crowd control, and being present at events that result in severe harm or loss of life. These experiences contribute to cumulative trauma, amplifying the susceptibility to developing post-traumatic stress disorder (PTSD).

The fifth edition of the Diagnostic and Statistical Manual of Mental Disorders (DSM-5; American Psychiatric Association [APA], 2013) defines PTSD as a disorder characterized by four symptom clusters: intrusion symptoms (distressing intrusive memories or images; flashbacks; nightmares); avoidance symptoms (e.g., avoiding reminders of the traumatic events, places, situations, conversations); negative alterations in cognitions and mood (e.g., persistent and exaggerated negative beliefs about oneself, others, or the world; feeling detached from others; diminished interest in activities); and marked alterations in arousal and reactivity (e.g., hypervigilance; difficulties with sleep and/or concentration). The symptoms last more than one month and cause distress and/or distress or impairment in the person's functioning (e.g., social; personal; occupational).

To have a better appreciation of the risk factors for psychological health problems and post-traumatic stress disorders, there is a need to appreciate a whole-life approach. For instance, when looking at the risk factors that lead to a post-traumatic stress disorder, there are pre-trauma risk factors (e.g., childhood adversity), peri-trauma risk factors (e.g., cumulative exposure to trauma and organizational stressors), and post-trauma risk factors (e.g., psychosocial stressors, moral injury, burnout, compassion fatigue).

Timely interventions play a crucial role, given that PTSD is recognized as a debilitating psychiatric condition. When not addressed promptly, PTSD can persist for extended periods, resulting in disruptions across an individual's cognitive, behavioral, emotional, and psychological functioning. Additionally, many individuals might encounter sub-clinical or mild yet impactful levels of PTSD symptoms, further contributing to instances of absenteeism, reduced productivity while present (presenteeism), elevated susceptibility to fatigue and burnout, and heightened challenges in managing workplace pressures, job-related stressors, and the cumulative effects of traumatic experiences.

Focus Areas of the Book

This book project is written by executives in policing.

Focus Areas of the Book Project include:

Trust in Leadership and Empathy
Leadership Building and Growth
Mental Health and Wellness in the Workplace
Mental Health Policies and Disability Management
Mental Health Education and Training
Mental Health Interventions
Strategies to Reduce Stigma
Self-Care and Resiliency

Strategies and Plans include:

Implementation of Organizational Changes
System Changes for Mental Health Needs
Education and Training Implementation
Disability Management Strategies
Proactive Preventative Measures for Burnout

Promoting Psychological Well-Being:

Systemic Innovative Changes presented are:

New Human Resource Practices
Education on Mental Health Intervention Skills
Developing Self-Efficacy Skills
Positive Proactive Coping Techniques
Coping with Psychological Distress

Benefits of Implementing Strategies include:

Reducing Mental Health Disabilities
Improving Psychological Well-Being
Enhancing Work Productivity and Engagement
Preventing the Recurrence of Mental Health Disabilities
Contributing to a Healthier Organization

Enhancing Organizational Resources by:

Work Autonomy and Empowerment
Training and Skill Building
Compensation Strategies for Well-Being
Increasing Productivity Within the Organization

Trust, Empathy, and Growth in Leadership

The book focuses on trust in leadership and leadership building on empathy and growth; mental health and wellness in the workplace; mental health policies and disability management; mental health education and training around mental health promotion; mental health interventions; strategies to reduce stigma; self-care and resiliency. Strategies and plans of action to implement organizational and system changes to better address mental health needs, mental health education and training, and disability management are detailed. The authors provide proactive preventative measures that help address burnout in the workplace.

Strategies for Organizational Change

Systemic innovative changes, and new human resource practices, in addition to implementing education on mental health intervention skills to help individuals develop self-efficacy skills, adopt positive proactive coping, and better cope with psychological distress and/or organizational stressors, can help reduce mental health disabilities, improve psychological well-being in the workplace, can help reduce the recurrence of mental health disabilities, improve work productivity and engagement, and contribute to a healthier organization. Organizational resources focused on work autonomy, training, and skills building, and compensation are part of strategies to help improve psychological well-being and increased productivity within the organization.

Post-traumatic Growth and Resilience

This book explores the realms of post-traumatic stress disorder and delves into the concept of post-traumatic growth (PTG) that can emerge in the wake of traumatic experiences. The pathways to achieving PTG are vividly illustrated, encompassing facets such as embracing a wholesome lifestyle, practicing self-nurturing, fortifying one's inner resilience, fostering a constructive self-perception, cultivating a supportive and optimistic social network, deriving meaning from adversity to ignite hope and purpose, and harnessing the power of transformation to distill wisdom and significance.

Furthermore, the book illuminates effective coping strategies designed to navigate life's stressors, fostering not only personal growth but also the mitigation of deleterious effects stemming from cumulative trauma exposure. For instance, techniques like identifying silver linings and cultivating gratitude, nurturing adept communication skills and enriching interpersonal bonds, engaging in rejuvenating activities that aid recovery, and nurturing hobbies that foster life satisfaction.

The acquisition of these proficiencies is imperative, given that psychosocial stressors, losses, and heightened tension frequently accompany the aftermath of trauma. These stressors can either exacerbate pre-existing challenges or contribute to an enhanced sense of well-being. Practical scenarios, such as media scrutiny and investigations, extended work hours, diminished sleep, or strains within family dynamics, aptly underscore the relevance of these acquired skills.

In addition to post-traumatic growth, the book as well as examples of biological resilience with coping strategies to help balance the nervous system and emotion regulation. Resilience is an ongoing interactive process between proactive and reactive resiliency. Education, mental health promotion, and early interventions can help with positive coping with stressors, in turn, leading to experiences of growth and cognitive rebuilding such as healthy formation of views of self, others, and the world.

Leadership for Post-traumatic Growth

This book on policing delves into the concept of leadership that fosters post-traumatic growth. Its aim is to act as a buffer against modifiable occupational risk factors and to alleviate the effects of potentially traumatic incidents. These incidents often contribute to the emergence, persistence, or worsening of mental health issues.

The book places emphasis on honing interpersonal and communication skills, enhancing organizational support and unity, discovering avenues for meaning and purpose, promoting positive self-development, and concentrating on proactive coping and well-being. It also encourages a willingness to seek assistance when needed.

Moreover, the book delves into strategies for cultivating a healthy and empathetic organizational culture. This culture is designed to cultivate trust in leadership and to establish a comprehensive action plan. This plan is geared towards strengthening organizational involvement, productivity, and overall well-being.

Dimensions of Recovery

The book illustrates the various dimensions of recovery, fostering well-being and recuperation across individual, organizational, and systemic levels.

Whitley and Drake (2010) have proposed a new dimensional approach to recovery by defining five broad recovery dimensions: clinical, existential, functional, social, and physical. Within its pages, a comprehensive view of recovery unfolds, spanning clinical recuperation (interventions to alleviate symptoms), physical rejuvenation (embracing a health-conscious lifestyle; prioritizing sleep), social revitalization (nurturing positive and robust social support), functional reinstatement (engaging in meaningful work tasks and roles), and spiritual renewal (cultivating personal growth and empowerment).

The most impactful mental health initiatives in workplaces are those that harmonize organizational, individual, and employee resources. These initiatives adopt a comprehensive and interconnected approach to caregiving, shaping both preventive strategies and intervention techniques.

In our pursuit of enhancing mental health within organizations, it is imperative to adopt a holistic and systemic care methodology. This is particularly crucial given the elevated risk of recurrent mental health conditions and the substantial costs associated with mental health-related disabilities.

Work Engagement and Organizational Performance

Work engagement is defined as a positive affective-motivational state related to well-being. It is characterized by vigor, dedication, and absorption (Schaufeli & Bakker, 2004). Employee engagement, the extent of commitment to an organization and its values and work satisfaction, has been found to be related to work performance, work productivity, reduced staff turnover, and employee satisfaction. A meta-analysis by Corbeanu et al. (2023) reported a correlation between the three components of work engagement (vigor, dedication, and absorption) and job performance. The authors indicate the importance of work engagement research in improving organizational performance.

The acknowledgment of work-related stress as a significant peril to both the workforce and working relationships stems from its connection to health issues, worker safety concerns, and disruptions in organizational productivity (Al-Makhaita et al., 2014; Jahromi & Hojat, 2014).

Part of designing a system approach to organizational health and safety includes building resiliency, mental health, and well-being pathways at both the individual/worker and organizational levels.

Both employee engagement and organizational engagement are found to be separate constructs. Organizational engagements are found to have stronger predictive utility than worker engagement when it comes to measuring certain organizational outcomes, for example, organizational citizenship behaviors that contribute to the organization's healthy functioning.

By fostering a foundation of trust in leadership and cultivating empathy within the workplace, an environment conducive to psychological safety emerges. This, in turn, facilitates the development of organizational engagement.

Individual and Organizational Approaches

Essential work resources encompassing support, training, education, and proper equipment play a vital role in effectively managing the equilibrium between work demands and personal responsibilities.

Furthermore, the presence of work autonomy, constructive feedback mechanisms, and nurturing relationships within the workplace, especially with supervisors, has been demonstrated to effectively mitigate the stress arising from the interplay between work and home life. Additionally, these factors contribute to the reduction of burnout risk.

While challenges such as fatigue, insufficient sleep, and the pursuit of a harmonious work-life balance persist, implementing systemic changes becomes imperative. Introducing adaptable work conditions, task modifications, and reimagined work structures stands to offer significant benefits in this regard. Targeted interventions directed towards workloads, including workload assessment and strategic adjustments to shift schedules, hold the potential to effectively address concerns surrounding fatigue and the delicate balance between work and personal life.

Establishing protective factors within the workplace is crucial for mitigating modifiable risk factors that contribute to occupational stressors. This, in turn, reduces the susceptibility to burnout and the potential for psychological and physical harm. One illustrative example of such protective factors is the concept of professional worthiness. This pertains to employees experiencing a sense of their work being genuinely esteemed and recognized. It involves the provision of constructive feedback and a prevailing perception that the tasks they undertake are harmonious with the overarching objectives and ideals of the organization. Consequently, this not only fosters a greater sense of job security but also facilitates personal and psychological growth. When job roles and responsibilities are perceived as meaningful and in alignment with an individual's training, passion, and the organization's purpose, the overall level of engagement and productivity is positively augmented.

Intrinsic motivation, professional worthiness, a sense of professional competence, and the feeling of being appreciated are amplified by the capacity to make choices and shoulder responsibilities. These elements collectively constitute work autonomy, which plays a crucial role in mitigating the likelihood of burnout. As a component of interventions aimed at managing workload, introducing diversity in job tasks to better align with training and personal interests can elevate motivation and personal development. Consequently, this fosters heightened productivity and elevated performance levels.

Promoting a thriving and positive workplace culture, along with leadership that prioritizes individuals, hinges on the imperative of providing comprehensive training and education in empathy. Navigating the nuances of empathy and its practical application can indeed present challenges. It becomes crucial to pinpoint specific skills integral to this training.

One such skill involves acquiring proficiency in active listening—an ability to truly hear and understand. Additionally, it entails recognizing and valuing the aspirations and objectives of employees. Demonstrating compassion in instances where personal life stressors are evident is equally vital. Moreover, vigilance in identifying signals of overwhelming workloads, characterized by exhaustion, an inability to cope, and a sense of helplessness, forms another key facet.

In essence, fostering a workplace that thrives on empathy and people-centric leadership necessitates equipping individuals with these discerning skills through comprehensive training initiatives.

Empathy within the workplace serves as a cornerstone for bolstering the social recovery aspect. Here, the establishment of robust and affirmative connections with both colleagues and supervisors assumes a central role in fostering recovery, well-being, and reintegration into work-related endeavors. Concurrently, this practice aids in the mitigation of workplace stigmatization, actively promoting the inclination to seek assistance when necessary. Consequently, these efforts contribute to the reduction of presenteeism, while seamlessly facilitating the process of resuming work responsibilities subsequent to a period of disability.

The authentic display of concern and reinforcement yields tangible benefits within the professional milieu. This is particularly evident in the form of safeguarding elements that fortify the workplace environment. The concept of resiliency, which encompasses the optimization of available resources, strengths, and positive attributes, as well as the presence of a dependable support infrastructure, is further elevated through the infusion of workplace empathy and the simultaneous reduction of entrenched stigmatization.

Strategies for Enhancing Well-Being

Apart from a range of organizational interventions, there exists a diverse array of individual approaches aimed at enhancing organizational health, well-being, and resilience.

The individual pathways to well-being play a pivotal role in minimizing stress-related consequences such as presenteeism, absenteeism, and staff turnover. Furthermore, they serve to elevate engagement and productivity, contributing to a healthier and more productive work environment.

The book also covers strategies for mitigating the detrimental effects of workplace stressors on health and well-being. It not only delves into personal approaches to health and stress management but also explores methods for bolstering the immune system and restoring equilibrium to the mind-body system. Moreover, adopting healthy lifestyle behaviors can further optimize the utilization of work and organizational resources.

Among these interventions are mindfulness-centered methods, stress management training, instruction in coping flexibility and emotional intelligence, as well as cognitive behavioral therapy. These techniques aid in acquiring proactive coping strategies, facilitating the effective management of stressors, and addressing symptoms of depression or anxiety. By fostering psychological well-being within the workplace, these strategies also serve to mitigate the chances of relapse or recurrence.

Emotional resilience and effective recovery time play crucial roles in replenishing energy and recuperating from demanding workloads that place both emotional and physical strains. This process aids in achieving relaxation and enhancing the sense of mastery over non-work-related endeavors. By mitigating fatigue and bolstering vitality, it facilitates psychological disengagement from work, fostering the cultivation of activities beyond professional obligations. Collectively, these practices contribute to diminishing the likelihood of compassion fatigue and burnout.

Focusing on cultivating flexibility involves fostering coping flexibility, which entails employing a range of coping strategies to effectively adapt to prevailing demands or stressors. These strategies encompass avoidant coping (steering clear of or overlooking the issue), approach coping (addressing and mitigating the stressor), problem-solving coping (resolving the underlying problem), and emotion-focused coping (managing emotional reactions to the stressor).

The book delves into the physical and mental well-being of officers, centering on strategies to reduce workplace stressors. Additionally, it explores methods to proactively address lifestyle choices that contribute to overall health improvement. Consequently, these efforts culminate in fostering a robust and thriving workforce.

Personal and professional resources could potentially act as a safeguard against workplace stressors; however, this isn't always the case due to mixed findings. Research does indicate the importance of addressing both occupational stressors and encouraging employees to cultivate proactive, positive strategies to enhance their well-being and manage psychophysiological responses effectively (Vleugels, 2022).

Regarding stress, the cognitive, physiological, behavioral, and emotional aspects encompass both manageable work-related stress factors (such as improved work organization, fatigue and workload management, decreased role ambiguity, beneficial social support, health-oriented initiatives, and interventions) and a wellness-oriented lifestyle (including improved sleep quality and healthy dietary practices). These factors collectively aid in effectively managing stress, thereby reducing its detrimental effects.

Replenishing an individual's cognitive, emotional, physiological, and behavioral health resources is essential to mitigate the detrimental impact of occupational stressors on both health and stress levels.

Within the pages of this book, a comprehensive exploration of strategies for enhancing well-being is undertaken. This involves tackling systemic shifts at the organizational level and advocating proactive methods to establish a wholesome approach to care. By embracing such an approach, the effective management of stress, the implementation of recovery initiatives, and the sustained cultivation of health and well-being are facilitated.

Contributing Authors

Grant Edwards, Retired Australian Police Commander, Head of Aspect Frontline, writes on "The Police Traumatic Stress Devil (PTSD)—The dichotomy of living with a Mental Health condition".

Dr. Ian Hesketh, PhD., Lead for Police Wellbeing in the UK at the College of Policing and the Senior Responsible Owner (SRO) for the National Police Wellbeing Service in the UK, works on "What do you know? Ensuring there is evidence to support meaningful wellbeing interventions in UK policing".

Dr Katrina Sanders MBBS FRACGP MPH, Fellow of the Royal Australian College of General Practitioners, Former Chief Medical Officer Australian Federal Police, addresses "A Biopsychosocial Approach to Officer Wellness".

Edmonton Police Chief Dale McFee, O.O.M., adds on "Not just a number—The intersections of individual trauma in police officers, offenders, and the community".

Andy Rhodes OBE QPM: Service Director National Police Well Being Service, NPCC & College of Policing England & Wales, works on "Why the personal resilience of police officers is vital to building community trust & confidence".

William D. Walsh, Lieutenant, Voorhees Police Department (NJ—USA), focuses on "Building Positive Partnerships as part of effective health and wellness strategies".

Ontario Provincial Police Commissioner Thomas Carrique, OOM, MA, details on "Revolutionizing Mental Health in Policing Through Resiliency and Transformational Leadership".

References

Ahola, K., Gould, R., Virtanen, M., Honkonen, T., Aromaa, A., & Lönnqvist, J. (2009). Occupational burnout as a predictor of disability pension: A population-based cohort study. *Occupational and Environmental Medicine, 66*, 284–290. https://doi.org/10.1136/oem.2008.038935

Al-Makhaita, H. M., Sabra, A. A., & Hafez, A. S. (2014). Predictors of work-related stress among nurses working in primary and secondary health care levels in Dammam, Eastern Saudi Arabia. *Journal of Family & Community Medicine, 21*, 79–84.

American Psychiatric Association. (2013). *Diagnostic and statistical manual of mental disorders* (5th ed.). American Psychiatric Association.

Boles, M., Pelletier, B., & Lynch, W. (2004). The relationship between health risks and work productivity. *Journal of Occupational and Environmental Medicine, 46*, 737–745.

Carleton, R. N., Afifi, T. O., Turner, S., Taillieu, T., Duranceau, S., LeBouthillier, D. M., Sareen, J., Ricciardelli, R., MacPhee, R. S., Groll, D., et al. (2018). Mental disorder symptoms among public safety personnel. *The Canadian Journal of Psychiatry, 63*, 54–64.

Carleton, R. N., Afifi, T. O., Taillieu, T., Turner, S., Krakauer, R., Anderson, G. S., MacPhee, R. S., Ricciardelli, R., Cramm, H. A., Groll, D., et al. (2019). Exposures to potentially traumatic events among public safety personnel in Canada. *Canadian Journal of Behavioural Science, 51*, 37–52.

Carleton, R. N., Afifi, T. O., Turner, S., Mason, J. E., Ricciardelli, R., McCreary, D. R., Vaughan, A., Anderson, G. S., Krakauer, R., Donnelly, E. A., Camp, R. D. II, Groll, D., Cramm, H. A., MacPhee, R. S., & Griffiths, C.T. (2020). Assessing the relative impact of diverse stressors among public safety personnel. *International Journal of Environmental Research & Public Health, 17*(4), 1234. https://doi.org/10.3390/ijerph17041234

Clement, S., Schauman, O., Graham, T., et al. (2015). What is the impact of mental health-related stigma on help-seeking? A systematic review of quantitative and qualitative studies. *Psychological Medicine, 45*, 11–27.

Cooper, C. L., & Marshall, J. (1976). Occupational sources of stress: A review of the literature relating to coronary heart disease and mental ill health. *Journal of Occupational and Organizational Psychology, 49*, 11–28.

Cooper, C. L., & Cartwright, S. (1994). Healthy mind—Healthy organization—A proactive approach to occupational stress. *Human Relations, 47*, 455–471.

Corbeanu, A., & Iliescu, D. (2023). The link between work engagement and job performance: A meta-analysis. *Journal of Personnel Psychology, 22*(3), 111–122. https://doi.org/10.1027/1866-5888/a000316

Dewa, C., van Weeghel, J., Joosen, M., & Brouwers, E. (2020). What could influence workers' decisions to disclose a mental illness at work? *The International Journal of Occupational and Environmental Medicine, 11*, 119–127. https://doi.org/10.34172/ijoem.2020.1870

Dewa, C. S., Hoch, J. S., Loong, D., Trojanowski, L., & Bonato, S. (2021). Evidence for the cost-effectiveness of return-to-work interventions for mental illness related sickness absences: A systematic literature review. *Journal of Occupational Rehabilitation, 31*(1), 26–40. https://doi.org/10.1007/s10926-020-09904-z. PMID: 32495150.

Evans-Lacko, S., & Knapp, M. (2016). Global patterns of workplace productivity for people with depression: Absenteeism and presenteeism costs across eight diverse countries. *Social Psychiatry and Psychiatric Epidemiology, 51*, 1525–1537.

Gaspar, F. W., Jolivet, D. N., Wizner, K., Schott, F., Dewa, C. S. (2020). Pre-existing and new-onset depression and anxiety among workers with injury or illness work leaves. *Journal of Occupational and Environmental Medicine, 62*(10), e567–e572. https://doi.org/10.1097/JOM.0000000000001985. PMID: 32769787; PMCID: PMC7537737.

Greenberg, P. E., Fournier, A. A., Sisitsky, T., Pike, C. T., Kessler, R. C. (2015). The economic burden of adults with major depressive disorder in the United States (2005 and 2010). *The Journal of Clinical Psychiatry, 76*(2), 155–162.

Hatch, D. J., Potter, G. G., Martus, P., Rose, U., & Freude, G. (2019). Lagged versus concurrent changes between burnout and depression symptoms and unique contributions from job demands and job resources. *Journal of Occupational Health Psychology, 24*(6), 617–628. https://doi.org/10.1037/ocp0000170. Epub 2019 Oct 10. PMID: 31599617; PMCID: PMC6878137.

Jahromi, K., & Hojat, M. (2014). The etiology of burnout syndrome and the levels of stress among nurses. *Jahrom University of Medical Sciences, 12*, 49–58.

Komarovskaya, I., Maguen, S., McCaslin, S. E., Metzler, T. J., Madan, A., Brown, A. D., Galatzer-Levy, I. R., Henn-Haase, C., & Marmar, C. R. (2011). The impact of killing and injuring others on mental health symptoms among police officers. *Journal of Psychiatric Research, 45*, 1332–1336.

Kubo, J., Goldstein, B. A., Cantley, L. F., et al. (2014). Contribution of health status and prevalent chronic disease to individual risk for workplace injury in the manufacturing environment. *Occupational and Environmental Medicine, 71*, 159–166.

Maslach, C., Schaufeli, W. B., & Leiter, M. P. (2001). Job burnout. *Annual Review of Psychology, 52,* 397–422. https://doi.org/10.1146/annurev.psych.52.1.397

McCreary, D. R., & Thompson, M. M. (2006). Development of two reliable and valid measures of stressors in policing: The operational and organizational police stress questionnaires. *International Journal of Stress Management, 13*, 494–518.

Meunier, S., Roberge, C., Coulombe, S., & Houle, J. (2019). Feeling better at work! Mental health self-management strategies for workers with depressive and anxiety symptoms. *Journal of Affective Disorders, 254*, 7-14. https://doi.org/10.1016/j.jad.2019.05.011. Epub 2019 May 6. PMID: 31082629.

Mojtabai, R., Olfson, M., Sampson, N. A., et al. (2011). Barriers to mental health treatment: results from the National Comorbidity Survey Replication. *Psychological Medicine, 41*, 1751–61.

Murray, C. J. L., Atkinson, C., Bhalla, K., Birbeck, G., Burstein, R., Chou, D., et al. (2013). The state of U.S. health, 1990–2010: Burden of diseases, injuries, and risk factors. *Journal of the American Medical Association, 310*, 591–608. https://doi.org/10.1001/jama.2013.13805

Oliphant, R. C. (2016). Healthy minds, safe communities: Supporting our public safety officers through a National Strategy for Operational Stress Injuries; Security, Standing Committee on Public Safety and National Security, Ed.; Standing Committee on Public Safety and National Security.

Schaufeli, W. B., Bakker, A. B., & Van Rhenen, W. (2009). How changes in job demands and resources predict burnout, work engagement, and sickness absenteeism. *Journal of Organizational Behavior, 30*, 893–917. https://doi.org/10.1002/job.595

Toch, H. (2002). *Stress in policing*. American Psychological Association.

Vleugels, W., Kilroy, S., Vervoort, L., Put, C., & De Witte, H. (2022). The combined influence of occupational stressors and individual lifestyle behaviors on employee stress complaints: Additive or interactive effects? *International Journal of Stress Management*, 29. https://doi.org/10.1037/str0000269

Whitley, R., & Drake, R. E. (2010). Recovery: A dimensional approach. *Psychiatric Services, 61*(12), 1248–1250. https://doi.org/10.1176/ps.2010.61.12.1248. PMID: 21123410.

World Health Organization. (2017). *Depression and other common mental disorders: Global health estimates* (pp. 1–24). World Health Organization.

Contents

Living with Post-traumatic Stress Injury (PTSI): The Power of Storytelling to Encourage Help-Seeking Barriers

Grant Edwards

Introduction

Police officers are often exposed to multiple traumatic events in their line of duty, such as child abuse and exploitation, severe assaults, murders, witnessing or investigating traffic accidents, suicides, and other violent incidents. They may also face being threatened or injured by a suspect or responding to natural disasters or terrorist acts. Police officers may experience cumulative trauma from repeated exposure to these stressful situations. These experiences can have a lasting impact on their mental health and well-being, leading to post-traumatic stress injuries (PTSI).

For the purpose of this paper, I will use the term PTSI. PTSI can impair the ability of police officers to perform their duties effectively and safely. It can affect their critical decision-making, their use of force, their communication skills, their teamwork, and their resilience (Violanti, 2018). It can also increase the risk of other problems, such as depression, anxiety, substance abuse, suicide, burnout, and marital conflict (Edwards, 2023). Therefore, it is important for police officers to recognize the signs and symptoms of PTSD or PTSI and seek help when needed. It is also important for police organizations to provide adequate support and resources for their officers who are exposed to traumatic events and who suffer from PTSD or PTSI.

Many police with PTSI may feel ashamed or afraid to seek help for their condition. They may think that they are weak, that no one will understand them, or that they will be judged or stigmatized. This may impact their ability and desire to access mental health services.

One way to overcome these barriers is to use storytelling as a tool for empowerment and connection. Storytelling is the act of sharing one's personal experiences and emotions with others in a narrative form. It can help people with PTSD to

G. Edwards (✉)
Helensvale, Queensland, Australia

K. Papazoglou, K. Kamkar (eds.), *Multi-faceted Approaches to Challenges and Coping in Law Enforcement*, https://doi.org/10.1007/978-3-031-62825-2_1

process their trauma, express their feelings, gain new perspectives, and find meaning and purpose in their lives. Storytelling can also help them reduce their sense of isolation and stigma and to build trust and empathy with others who have gone through similar experiences. By telling their stories, they can reclaim their voice and identity and inspire hope and resilience in themselves and others.

I will use my own lived experience with a post-traumatic stress injury to share how storytelling helped me on my journey toward better mental health and helped others by giving them confidence they can come forward, acknowledge their condition, and seek help.

Living with Post-traumatic Stress

Policing isn't a career for everyone. It takes a particular person to be exposed day in, day out to the continual and cumulative stresses the profession presents. Stress and trauma experienced by police officers in the line of duty can have negative effects on officers' health and well-being. Police officers are expected to perform well and make the right decisions under extreme stress. What other job requires you to be in a constant state of hypervigilance and alertness yet be a counselor, a social worker, a lawyer, or a prison warden? What other profession authorizes you to take a person's liberty, or potentially use deadly force, but then mandates that you attempt to save the person's life that has just tried to kill you? What job causes you to wonder whether you will come home to your loved ones after you bid them farewell every day as you head off to work?

As a result, the prevalence of mental illness, specifically PTSI, among law enforcement officers is increasing despite genuine intent by leaders, policymakers, and practitioners to combat this public health epidemic (Kamkar et al., 2020).

Post-traumatic stress injury (PTSI) is a term that describes a range of mental health issues that can affect police officers who are exposed to potentially traumatic situations in their work.

PTSI differs from PTSD as a biological nature of the injury rather than the psychological disorder because of the changes in the nervous system that occur after exposure to a traumatic event. PTSD is a mental health condition that is listed in the DSM-5, while PTSI is not yet recognized as an official diagnosis. However, both PTSI and PTSD can cause similar symptoms (Wallace et al., 2020). The major difference is how people perceive and cope with their condition. Some experts suggest that using the term PTSI can reduce the stigma and shame that often accompany PTSD and encourage people to seek treatment. However, some experts suggest that using the term post-traumatic stress injury (PTSI) can reduce the stigma and shame that often accompany PTSD and encourage people to seek treatment. It is argued that PTSI is a more accurate and compassionate way to describe the impact of trauma on the brain and body and that it can help people see their condition as something that can heal and improve over time (Lipov, 2023).

Police with PTSI may experience the following:

- An intrusion of thoughts: Someone with PTSD may experience repeated, involuntary memories, distressing dreams, or flashbacks of their traumatic event.
- Avoidance: The person may avoid certain people, activities, places, or objects that remind them of the traumatic event they experienced.
- Altered thinking and mood: Some people with PTSD have difficulties remembering essential aspects of a traumatic event, negative thoughts, and feelings. This leads to a distorted belief not only about themselves but others. Additionally, there may be a distorted belief surrounding the cause of the event leading to self-blame or the blaming of others. A person may also feel less connected to activities previously enjoyed and feel detached and estranged from others.
- Altered arousal and reactivity: Arousal and reactive symptoms may include outbursts, irritation, reckless behavior, suspicion, concentration issues, and more.

They may feel numb, detached, or hopeless about the future. They may also have difficulty sleeping, concentrating, or controlling their emotions. They may be constantly on edge, alert for signs of danger, or easily startled. Symptoms can affect those suffering with PTSI that can interfere with daily functioning and quality of life for a long time after the traumatic event (Asalgoo et al., 2016; Pitts et al., 2022).

Police organizations, the government, and the public expect police officers not only to be healthy but also to maintain high performance levels in the line of duty (Papazoglou & Tuttle, 2018). Over the length of a 30–35-year career, it is estimated that police officers might be exposed to at least 900 potentially traumatic incidents (Rudofossi, 2009).

The prevalence of PTSI in police officers has been the subject of a large and highly variable empirical literature. A systematic review of international studies found that the prevalence of PTSI in police ranged from 4% to 41%, depending on the sample, the measure, and the definition of PTSD (Wagner et al., 2020).

Police with PTSI may have persistent and intrusive memories of the event, which can cause them to relive it repeatedly. They may also avoid anything that reminds them of the trauma, such as places, people, or situations. They may feel numb, detached, or hopeless about the future. They may also have increased arousal, which means they are constantly on edge, easily startled, or angry. These symptoms can also interfere with their daily functioning and work and personal relationships. Police with PTSI may feel different emotions depending on the type and severity of their trauma, their personality, their coping skills, and their social support.

Some common feelings that I experienced were as follows:

- Fear: I felt afraid of the event happening again or of losing control or harming myself or others. I also felt like I was being judged or rejected by others because of my condition.
- Guilt: I blamed myself for the event, for surviving while others did not, and for not being able to prevent or stop my trauma. I also feel guilty for having negative thoughts or feelings about the events that were affecting me.
- Anger: I felt angry at myself and the situation that caused my trauma and being unable to cope. I initially felt resentful toward others who did not understand or support me.

- Sadness: At times I felt sad about the loss of my life as it was, safety, and innocence that resulted from the trauma. I also felt depressed, hopeless, and suicidal.
- Shame: At times, I felt ashamed of my symptoms, such as having nightmares and panic attacks. I also feel embarrassed about needing help and showing weakness.
- Disgust: I felt disgusted and repulsed by certain sights and sounds that reminded me of my trauma.

Police officers who are exposed to various traumatic events and stressors in their line of duty may use maladaptive behaviors to cope with their symptoms and emotional pain. Maladaptive behaviors are actions that are harmful or ineffective in reducing stress or solving problems. Examples of maladaptive behaviors that I used included the use of alcohol or drug abuse, eating disorders, self-harm, gambling, and suicidal thoughts. These behaviors may worsen their mental and physical health, impair their work performance, and damage their relationships.

Maladaptive behaviors are actions that prevent people from adapting, adjusting, or participating in different aspects of life. Such actions are intended to help relieve or avoid stress, but they are often disruptive and may contribute to increased distress, discomfort, and anxiety. People who suffer from post-traumatic stress disorder (PTSD) may develop maladaptive behaviors as a result of their traumatic experiences (Vogt, 2012).

Maladaptive behaviors are not signs of weakness or failure. They are understandable responses to traumatic events that may have helped people survive in the past. However, they are not helpful in the present and may cause more harm than good (Dixon, 2021).

The Importance of Storytelling

Storytelling is the process of sharing one's personal experiences and emotions with others in a safe and supportive environment. Storytelling can have many benefits for people with PTSI, such as reducing the sense of isolation and loneliness, increasing the sense of self-worth and empowerment, enhancing the coping skills and resilience, and promoting the healing process by releasing the emotional burden and trauma stored in the body and mind.

Storytelling can take many forms, such as writing, speaking, drawing, painting, singing, dancing, or any other creative expression. Storytelling can be done individually or in groups, with family, friends, peers, professionals, or strangers. Storytelling can be done online or offline, in formal or informal settings. The choice of how and with whom to share one's story depends on one's personal preferences and goals.

The most important thing is to find a way of storytelling that feels comfortable and meaningful for oneself. Storytelling is not a onetime event, but a continuous journey of exploration and discovery. Storytelling is not a cure for PTSI, but a tool for recovery and growth.

Research from the field of narrative psychology shows a distinctive link between narratives and well-being (Adler et al., 2016). Talking about emotionally significant events is a basic activity in human relationships and plays an integral role in the recovery process (Murphy, 2021). Storytelling—or narrative—is fundamental to how we think and make meaning of the world. Whether we realize it or not, stories are at the center of everything we do. How we tell our stories helps our mood, self-image, and the influence we have on others (Rutledge, 2016).

Police officers are storytellers by nature (Gallagher, 2019). Police stories are an important part of the "meaning-making structure" in policing and often convey particular power well beyond the limitations of formal organizational or agency policy (Kurtz et al., 2019). The importance of storytelling within police culture cannot be understated (Reiner & Newburn, 2007). Skillful storytelling helps police understand the essence of complex concepts and ideas in meaningful and often personal ways (Suzuki et al., 2018). Sharing experiences and emotions through storytelling can be a powerful tool for healing and processing trauma. In a culture where mental health is often stigmatized, storytelling can help reduce the shame and isolation that many individuals feel. It can also provide a sense of connection and understanding with others who may have similar experiences. Furthermore, when someone listens to a story, their brain waves start to synchronize with those of the storyteller. Reading a narrative activates brain regions involved in deciphering or imagining a person's motives and perspective, and research has found storytelling can be a way for individuals to gain insights into their own mental health and develop a greater sense of self-awareness (Renken, 2020).

My Lived Experience Story

Never in my wildest dreams did I think I'd ever become a mental health statistic. In 2014, I was diagnosed with complex post-traumatic stress and unipolar depression. I would become a law enforcement officer who tried to take their own life.

I had always known I would become a law enforcement officer. It was in my blood. Like many who join, it was my purpose in life and it became my identity. I wanted to make a difference for my family, my community, and my country.

On the 11th of August 1985, my life forever changed. I joined the Australian Federal Police (AFP). From the time I entered the academy, they subjected me to an overabundance of information that was necessary to make me into the best law enforcement officer I could be. They bought to the peak of physical fitness, subjected me to a battery of physical testing, and taught about the law and how to enforce it. They drilled me on the organizational procedures, governance, and protocols that I was required to adhere to. I spent countless hours learning and practicing self-defense to ensure I could stay safe. Every week they instructed me on the use of force techniques, how to deescalate violent situations, and the effective use of handcuffs, batons, and OC spray. They allocated a great deal of time to train me in the education and use of executing lethal force. I had become skilled in maintaining neutrality with my emotions and instructed on how to remain impassive in difficult and critical situations. They shaped me to distrust and question everything and never take an answer, event, or situation at face value. The deficit of distrust becomes so strong that it's pervasive in your life.

The potential of being psychologically affected by the work was never addressed or taught. I was about to embark upon, and how could I educate and prepare myself to deal with the stressors of the job. I had known "the job" was tough. I had two uncles in law enforcement, and I saw how the job affected their health, but we never spoke about it—just acknowledged it and moved on.

In my early days, work was busy. I would work long hours, sometimes 24 plus hours straight to the point of absolute exhaustion. Shift work meant I developed unhealthy sleep habits, altered my nutritional behaviors, and stopped exercising. I would spend disproportionate amounts of time away from home due to last-minute assignments, missing holidays, and many pivotal events like my children's birthdays and milestone events. Over the years, my stress and anxiety levels crept ever higher and higher.

Throughout my career, I was verbally abused, physically assaulted, spat at, and bitten and had urine and feces thrown at me. I suffered from cuts, abrasions, sprains, and broken bones. I dealt with horrendous crimes, homicides, rapes, assaults, and fatal motor vehicle accidents. I saw other human beings beheaded and children exposed to chemical weapons. I would remove infants suffering welts and sores from a flea infested, maggot ridden homes. I saw children, some as young as 6 months of age, horrendously abused, sexually assaulted, and molested to satisfy the inhuman desires of some.

I would find myself in hospital operating theaters with doctors trying to save the life of a drug courier who attempted to internally import drugs through the border. His "friends" were so drugged they used the chord of an iron to try to electrically jump-start his heart after he had died.

I was deployed to hostile environments in Timor-Leste and Afghanistan. I would be forcefully removed from a vehicle at gunpoint by the local military and attacked by Taliban insurgents in Kabul, who detonated their bomb vests and indiscriminately shot at anyone or anything that moved.

I would regularly be ridiculed, patronized, and mocked before your peers, the jury and judiciary, without the opportunity of rebuttal. Worst of all, criminals would physically and psychologically threaten and intimidate me and my family.

At times, I was bullied, threatened, and unnecessarily ridiculed by peers and my superiors. I preferred to focus on my physical health outside of work and rarely would involve myself in social events. Back in those days, the culture determined it was far more acceptable to be out having a lengthy lunch or plying yourself with alcohol than it was to work toward being fit and healthy.

I accepted that this was what it was.

In late 2013, I returned from a 12-month deployment to Afghanistan. It was around this time I started experiencing physical and psychological problems. The best way I could describe what was happening to me was "I felt odd.". "Things were not right." I had become increasingly tense, impatient, irritated, intolerant, and angry. The most innocuous noise caused me to jump and twitch. I noticed I was becoming hypervigilant, abnormally alert to potential danger or threats to where I was unable to control it. My mind was turning to a mush of confusing thoughts, obscuring my ability to think logically and coherently. I had become a prisoner in my mind without a key to leave. I avoided friends, colleagues, and family and became a recluse. Migraine headaches and muscle and joint aches were immobilizing me, and my stomach was in a constant state of churn. I become so afraid to sleep because of the intrusive dreams playing on a never-ending repeat cycle that fatigue consumed my waking hours. I turned to alcohol and over-the-counter drugs, a futile effort to relax and help me sleep. Addiction would be the logical next step.

Despite this, I never thought I was suffering from a mental health issue. I would be referred to a plethora of medical specialists to provide me with answers to why I was feeling and acting the way I was. They subjected me to a plethora of tests, poked and prodded beyond belief.

My mind could not reconcile what was happening to me. I was the cop that was supposed to be tough and calm. I was also the fit and healthy former elite athlete who represented his country in five different sports and played American football at the University of Hawaii. I was also the strongman who could pull trucks, buses, trams, airplanes, sailing ships, locomotive trains, and huge mining trucks.

My health continued to decline. I had become out of control to where internal voices would tell me I was a burden to my family and loved ones, an imposition to my colleagues and friends, and an embarrassment to myself. It seemed everything I had worked for throughout my life had become worthless, just like I felt I was.

During my deployments overseas, I contracted several exotic diseases like tick paralysis, chikungunya, dengue fever, and schistosomiasis that left me with lifelong debilitating consequences. I would be diagnosed with gastritis, gastroesophageal disease and reflux, paraesthesia, abnormal obstructive lung pattern, tinnitus, Wills-Ekbom disease (restless leg syndrome), and temporomandibular joint (TMJ) dysfunction. I would eventually also be diagnosed with myalgic encephalomyelitis (chronic fatigue syndrome)/fibromyalgia and Barret's esophagus.

I had become highly hypervigilant and suffered with disassociation, involuntary trigger responses in public, constant allergies, and unexplained skin rashes. My appetite reduced, migraine/headaches escalated, and my joints constantly ached. The brain fog and confusion were substantial, as were my dizziness, fatigue, and lethargy.

Because of the adversarial insurance processes in Australia, I would be forced to see over 20 medical doctors and specialists with most of my insurance claims denied. I was diagnosed by one insurance specialist medical advisor as "obese" whom he stated was the primary reason for some conditions. Like many in my situation, the insurance provider placed the onus on me to prove my illnesses and their connection to my work, which I was not trained or experienced in.

At my worst, I was taking up to 14 medications daily, several of which were to counteract the side effects of existing medications. I was numbed to the point where I thought I was just surviving and not thriving.

Depending on the severity of my condition, I was in bed or couch bound for between 24 h and 4 days. My mental health declined rapidly, and I regularly ruminated with suicidal ideations.

I would accept that I was the only one who could drive my internal change. Once I gave myself permission to "own" my situation, things changed. I would accept that I'd never be the same person I was before my injury. I acknowledged I had been faking being well, not faking being sick. I had to regain control over my life and jettison the vulnerability I felt, my feelings of inadequacy, fear, and shame for having PTSD. I had to overcome the inherent distrust, skepticism, and cynicism that had been drilled into me as a police officer.

My trauma would consume my life if left unaddressed. I would accept that treatment is nasty, grueling, draining, and never ending. I accepted that there is no lineal process for healing and that it is an individual process.

However, I hadn't devoted time and effort to the positives that accompanied my PTSD. Yes, positives. Who would have thought? I now acknowledge that I am a survivor, not cured, as I firmly believe there is no cure for PTSD, just that we individually learn to live with it as best we can. Importantly, I knew I was not alone and no longer would I allow myself to be a hostage to PTSD. Through my therapy, I've learned so much about myself I never knew before. I developed a renewed appreciation and meaning for life. I developed a healthy appreciation for the impact family and loved ones have on my journey to better mental health.

Coping Mechanisms That Worked for Me

I realized very early in my journey that no one program, system, or treatment is universal. The treatment of post-traumatic stress disorder must be individually focused.

Dealing with stress requires conscious effort (Mitrousi et al., 2013). Self-help and coping skills are an integral part of the recovery process. Good coping takes practice and can be deployed through many mechanisms, including coping mechanisms, self-help strategies, and symptom management (US Department of Veterans Affairs, 2023). Coping is defined as the thoughts and behaviors mobilized to manage internal and external stressful situations (Algorani & Gupta, 2022) as opposed to the use of more maladaptive strategies such as avoidance, pseudo-planning, fantasizing, and impulsive and depressive behavior (Biro et al., 1997).

What follows are the elements that have worked for me.

Become the Center of Your Universe

Although I did not realize it when I was first diagnosed with PTSD, I was in survival mode. What that meant for me was everything else in my universe had to take a back seat to me, my health and my survival. Concentrating on myself might sound egocentric and quite self-centered, and it is. Being self-centered has always been a foreign concept to me and counterintuitive. We are expected to always put others first when we do our job. It took me some time to break that pattern of thinking. I now know, though, that it's hugely important to make sure that no matter what happens, I always tried to put myself first and keep my self-worth above that of others. I knew if I didn't do this, I would fail in my recovery processes and be unable to be at my best but be able to help and support my family, colleagues, and friends.

Educate Yourself

Struggling with PTSI is complex and, like many, I initially did so in isolation, finding it hard to reach out and harder to acknowledge what I was going through. In fact, most of my friends and colleagues did not even realize I was struggling with PTSI. I was even ignorant of the symptoms and processes of PTSI, so one of the first actions I immersed myself in knowledge. I needed to know how best to educate myself on the behaviors, symptoms, impact, and treatment options. By learning about my condition, I can articulate more clearly and explain to others what is happening to me. It also allowed me to better understand why I was behaving and reacting the way I was.

Educating myself on my mental health condition was so important for many reasons. I was acutely aware of the need for self-health management. I knew if I didn't make proactive efforts to look after myself and continue to neglect my mind, body, and spirit, then I would be doomed to a life of poor health. It helped me understand my symptoms and how they affect my mood, thinking, and behavior. Knowing what I was experiencing made me feel less alone and more empowered to cope with my challenges.

I was able to find the best treatment options for my condition, as it is a very individual process. Different mental health conditions may require different types of therapies, medications, or lifestyle changes. Learning about the pros and cons of each option helped me make informed decisions about my care.

By doing so, it can help you communicate better with my health professionals, family, and friends. Being able to explain what I was going through and what I needed improved your relationships and my support network. It also helped me advocate for myself and my rights as a person with a mental health condition.

My education process also helped me reduce the stigma and discrimination that was forefront in my thinking process. Mental health conditions are common and treatable, but many people still face negative attitudes and stereotypes because of their condition. Educating yourself and others can help challenge these myths and promote a more positive and respectful view of mental health.

There are many sources of information about mental health conditions, such as books, websites, podcasts, videos, or support groups. However, not all sources are reliable or accurate. My advice is you should always check the credibility of the source and the evidence behind the information. Some trustworthy sources I found useful are as follows:

- Healthdirect—this website provides information on various mental health conditions and their causes, symptoms, diagnosis, and treatment. It also offers links to other helpful resources and services.
- Mayo Clinic—this website offers comprehensive information on different types of mental illnesses, their signs and causes, how they are diagnosed and treated, and how to cope and support someone with a mental illness.
- Your doctor or mental health professional—the most important source as they can give you personalized advice on your condition and the best treatment options for you. They can also refer you to other specialists or support services if needed.

Educating yourself on your mental health condition was a valuable step toward my recovery and well-being. It helped me take charge of my health and work toward living the best life I could.

Be Honest About Your Needs

It took me some time, but being honest about what I was going through and articulating it to family and loved ones was essential, especially in what they can do to help.

Being honest about my mental health needs is important for me and for those around me. It helps me to cope with stress, to seek support when I need it, and to avoid misunderstandings or conflicts. I don't have to hide or pretend that everything is fine when it's not. I can express my feelings and thoughts in a respectful and constructive way. I can also respect the boundaries and needs of others and ask for their respect in return. Being honest about my mental health needs is a sign of strength, not weakness.

Being honest about your mental health needs is important for several reasons. First, it can help you get the appropriate support and treatment that you deserve. Second, it can reduce the stigma and shame that often surrounds mental health issues. Third, it can empower you to take charge of your own well-being and recovery. By being honest about your mental health needs, you are showing respect and compassion for yourself and others.

It was important that I ask them to be patient, but equally I had to be patient with myself. Setting and maintaining healthy boundaries around time or personal space can be important in relationships. Learning how to trust people and asking for help can be significant obstacles but are very important—especially with those who care for us most.

Seek Professional Help

Having a professionally trained person available to offer support and guidance in my recovery is a key element to long-term success. It helped me understand and cope with my emotions, thoughts, and behaviors and improve well-being. Professional help also provided me with support, guidance, and skills to deal with life's challenges and achieve my goals.

Find someone you feel comfortable with, whom you find trustworthy and knowledgeable, and be consistent in attending your sessions. Talking with a therapist originally felt a bit intimidating, but once I overcame the trust deficit issues and found the right therapist for me, I have continued to improve when struggling with PTSD. Learning healthy and effective coping skills is helping me live a fuller life and manage some symptoms I'm experiencing with PTSI.

Deep Breathing

It may sound silly, but many people do not breathe properly. I didn't. Natural breathing involves your diaphragm, a large muscle in your abdomen. When you breathe in, your belly should expand. When you breathe out, your belly should fall.

Over time, people forget how to breathe this way and instead use their chest and shoulders. This causes short and shallow breaths, which can increase stress and anxiety.

I was first alerted to this by my physiotherapist, whom I was seeking for a completely different problem. She helped me relearn how to breathe deeply from my diaphragm, which has an immediate impact in lowering my heart rate and reducing the impact of stress.

Deep breathing is a technique that involves inhaling deeply and exhaling slowly, using the diaphragm muscle. Deep breathing can have many benefits for your health and well-being, such as the following:

- Reducing stress and anxiety by activating the parasympathetic nervous system, which slows down the heart rate and lowers blood pressure
- Improving oxygen delivery to the cells and organs by expanding the lungs and clearing out toxins
- Enhancing focus and concentration by calming the mind and increasing blood flow to the brain
- Promoting better sleep quality by relaxing the body and mind before bedtime
- Supporting recovery from exercise by easing muscle tension and inflammation

How I practice deep breathing is to

- Sit or lie down comfortably and place one hand on my chest and one on your abdomen.

- Breathe in slowly through your nose, feeling my abdomen rise as I fill my lungs with air.
- Breathe out slowly through my mouth, feeling my abdomen fall as I empty my lungs of air.
- Repeat this cycle for a few minutes, focusing on my breath and letting go of any thoughts or distractions.

The good thing is I can practice deep breathing anytime I feel stressed, tired, or overwhelmed, or as part of your daily routine to improve your health and well-being.

Practicing simple deep breathing exercises to improve your breathing and combat anxiety doesn't cost and can be done anywhere and anytime. I have little stickers strategically in my car, office, and home that prompts me to take a micro-moment to stop, calm myself, and breathe.

Progressive Muscle Relaxation

Using relaxation exercises can be an effective way to reduce your stress and anxiety. I had learned this technique when I was an elite athlete to relax my muscles. However, until recently I did not know how important this technique was to lower stress and anxious muscles. Progressive muscle relaxation focuses on alternating between tensing and relaxing different muscle groups throughout the body following a body scanning process. As ironic as it sounds, complete relaxation of your muscles can only be achieved by first going to the other extreme (i.e., by tensing your muscles).

Mindfulness

One of the first techniques I learned following my diagnosis was mindfulness. Mindfulness is a state of awareness and attention to the present moment, without judgment or reactivity. Mindfulness can be cultivated through various practices, such as meditation, breathing exercises, yoga, or simply paying attention to one's sensations, thoughts, and emotions. Mindfulness can have many benefits for one's well-being, such as reducing stress, enhancing focus, improving mood, and fostering compassion. Mindfulness is not a religion or a philosophy, but a skill that anyone can learn and apply in their daily life.

I found using mindfulness was very helpful for calming my anxiety. Mindfulness has been around for ages. It taught me to be in touch with and being aware of the present moment. It helped me loosen my thoughts and ruminations that were stuck in my head, where I was caught up in the anxiety and worries of daily life, always looking forward or backward without stopping to feel the moment.

Cognitive Behavioral Therapy

Cognitive behavioral therapy (CBT) is a type of psychotherapy that helped me change my thoughts and behaviors that was causing them distress. CBT is based on the idea that our thoughts, emotions, and actions are interconnected and that by identifying and modifying negative or irrational thoughts, we can improve our mood and cope better with life's challenges.

CBT is a structured and goal-oriented therapy that involved a limited number of sessions with my therapist who helped identify my problems and goals and taught me the skills and strategies to deal with them.

CBT is an evidence-based therapy that has been shown to be effective for many people. However, CBT is not a one-size-fits-all approach, and it may not work for everyone. Some people may find CBT too challenging or confronting or may not feel comfortable with the therapist or the format of the therapy. CBT also requires active participation and commitment from the client, which may not suit everyone's preferences or abilities.

Self-Monitoring

Another key early lesson I learned was to self-monitor. Self-monitoring can be a helpful way of getting a handle on your anxiety symptoms. We are all creatures of habit. We often go about our day without thinking, being unaware of much that goes on around us.

Self-monitoring is a key component of self-management, which is the ability to cope with a chronic condition like PTSI. Self-monitoring involves measuring one's own vital signs, symptoms, behaviors, or psychological well-being, interpreting the data, and being proactive in adjusting one's medication, treatment, lifestyle, or help-seeking behavior accordingly. Self-monitoring has a significant benefit for my health and well-being. I use biometric wearables such as Fitbit and Whoop that measures various physiological signals from the human body, such as heart rate, blood pressure, skin temperature, and oxygen saturation. These devices can be worn on different parts of the body, such as wristbands, smartwatches, earbuds, or glasses. Biometric wearables can be used for various purposes, such as fitness tracking, health monitoring, stress management, or personal identification.

Self-monitoring also helps me increase knowledge and awareness of my condition and its management and enhances self-efficacy and empowerment by giving me more control and independence over my health. It also helps me identify triggers and coping strategies for my PTSI.

Distraction

Distraction techniques are coping skills that help me shift my attention away from unpleasant or overwhelming emotions or sensations. These techniques can be cognitive, behavioral, or physiological. Distraction is anything you do to temporarily take your attention off a powerful emotion. Purposeful use of distraction techniques can be of benefit in coping with emotions that are strong or feel uncomfortable, such as anxiety and fear. It doesn't matter what it might be; the point is to use whatever works for you.

Unknown to me I have always used sport as a distraction. Whether it be walking, running, or undertaking one of my favorite sports, when I'm doing an activity, I'm completely in the moment and totally distracted from everything else around me.

Some other examples of distraction techniques I use are counting, doodling, breathing, imagining, coloring in, or reaching out to others. Distraction techniques are not a cure for mental health problems, but a strategy to manage them along with other therapies. In the past, I used unhealthy or maladaptive distraction techniques, such as reliance on alcohol and over-the-counter medications to distract me, which can be harmful and difficult to stop.

I've also found treatments like infrared sauna, floatation magnesium pools, massage, and acupuncture as very helpful treatment and distraction activities with huge overall health benefits for me.

The Six Pillars of Health

Many years ago, as I began my journey toward being the best version of me, I discovered the six pillars of health. Although they can vary in structure, they are mostly quite similar, and, again, it's best to design your own based on your specific needs. Like every structure built in the world, without strong and stable pillars, most would collapse into rubble. It's the same for me. These pillars guided me and produced meaningful progress in how I felt. By providing me with the tools to look within and establish what my body needed, I could respond to the stress and chaos of work and life. With these tools, I could aim at building self-mastery and self-trust to create a vibrant well-being that was tailor-made for me.

The processes I now use and stand by in my healing processes are based on my own designed six pillars of health.

Nutrition and Nourishment

Nutrition embodies the concept of food as medicine and that what we put into our system can heal or hurt us. In the fast paced, hectic, and stressful policing environment, I fell into the trap of continually reaching for a simple and easy food that could be eaten on the run. In our time poor career, I often preferred the convenience of highly processed, simple fast foods to quell my hunger pains while continuing to push through meeting my never-ending work obligations.

At the most basic level, nourishment is about eating real, whole foods—foods that don't need an ingredient list. I try and feed my body with a variety of amazing foods that come from the earth. I want to eat all the colors of the rainbow and consume food that isn't contaminated with pesticides and chemicals or highly processed.

I learned it is important to remove foods that are toxic to my body—foods that I was allergic or sensitive to, foods that were full of chemicals that were difficult for my body to digest properly, and foods with ingredients that I didn't recognize.

Finally, nourishment also includes how you eat: To maximize the benefits, I aim to eat mindfully, so that my body is in the "rest and digest" mode, able to absorb all the amazing nutrients I am eating. Take the time to truly enjoy your food by slowing down when you eat, giving yourself a well-earned break away from the turmoil of work and life. I know this is almost impossible when you're on the run as a police officer from job to job or meeting a pressured time commitment handed to you by the boss. However, by setting a little time aside each week and meal prepping, I found I was far more likely to consume more healthy food, rather than relying on takeaway or a convenience meal.

Movement

You notice I haven't titled this pillar exercise. My experience is that this title alone scares many off because of its association with hard effort. Although movement refers to how you exercise and move your body, it's not about taking a vigorous class, a 5-km run, or a heavy gym session. It's just about being active.

Movement is important to manage your mental health because it can have positive effects on your mood, cognition, and well-being. Movement can include any physical activity that you enjoy, such as walking, running, dancing, yoga, or playing sports. Movement can help you cope with stress, anxiety, and depression by releasing endorphins, which are natural chemicals that make you feel good. Movement can also improve your self-esteem, confidence, and body image by making you stronger, fitter, and more flexible. Movement can also enhance your brain function by increasing blood flow, oxygen, and nutrients to your brain cells. Movement can also stimulate the growth of new brain cells and connections, which can improve your memory, learning, and creativity. Movement can also help you sleep better by regulating your circadian rhythm, which is your body's natural clock that tells you when to wake up and when to sleep. Movement can also help you socialize with others by giving you opportunities to meet new people, join a group or a team, or share a common interest. Movement can also help you have fun and enjoy life by providing you with a sense of accomplishment, satisfaction, and joy.

We were made to move and be active; however, our lives are becoming increasingly sedentary. Sitting is now referred to by many medical practitioners as the new “smoking” in terms of its impact on our health. Importantly, this pillar is about integrating movement into your daily life in a way that is sustainable, fun, and relaxing. It allows you to have a capable body to carry you through your career and life.

We have to reframe how we think of exercise from being a chore to a practice, just like meditation. Exercise is no longer a “nice to have” but a necessity of life. Learn what kind of movement energizes you and truly feels good in your body, rather than draining you or leaving you so uninspired. It is difficult to continue. Developing a consistent movement practice allows you to be more genuine in your exercise endeavor and reclaim it as part of your life, rather than something to achieve or to an ideal that is false to your true happiness.

Stress and Fatigue Management

An unfortunate part of the law enforcement job is that we are required to be “on” all day, every day, and our nervous systems take a toll. The elevated stress response affects every area of health in the body. Researchers like Professor John Violanti, an internationally known expert on law enforcement stress and law enforcement veteran who served as a New York State Police trooper for 23 years, and Dr. Kevin Gilmartin, a retired law enforcement officer from Arizona, USA, and a behavioral scientist specializing in law enforcement and public safety related issues, detail throughout their research.

Stress and fatigue management is important in managing police mental health because it can help prevent or reduce the negative effects of stress on physical and mental well-being. Police officers face various sources of stress in their work. These stressors can impair their judgment, mood, adaptability, and sense of threat and increase their risk of developing health problems such as heart disease, stomach disorders, depression, burnout, post-traumatic stress disorder (PTSD), alcohol abuse, and suicidal behavior.

Stress and fatigue management can help police officers cope with the demands of their job and maintain their health and performance. Some strategies I have used for stress and fatigue management include scheduling vacations and personal downtime, seeing a doctor regularly for checkups, sharing the workload, and reducing the amount of overtime. I have sought professional financial advice to ensure I am living within my financial means. By implementing these strategies and others I have articulated in this paper, police officers can enhance their resilience and well-being in the face of stress and fatigue.

Learning to wind down is about learning what works for you.

Sleep Hygiene

Anyone who has worked in law enforcement knows that sleep falls to the bottom of the list in terms of priority. I can recall in my younger years as a police detective working beyond 24 h straight and occasionally going beyond 40 h without sleep. Being so sleep deprived is both physically and psychologically damaging.

Why is sleep hygiene important in managing police mental health? Sleep hygiene refers to the habits and practices that promote good quality and regular sleep. It includes factors such as having a comfortable and quiet sleeping environment, avoiding caffeine and alcohol before bed, following a consistent bedtime routine, and limiting screen time prior to sleep. Sleep hygiene is important for everyone, but especially for police officers who face high levels of stress, trauma, and shift work that can disrupt their sleep patterns and affect their mental health.

Sleep is essential for maintaining physical and mental well-being. It helps the body and brain to recover from the day's activities, regulate emotions, consolidate memories, and enhance cognitive functions. When police officers do not get enough or good quality sleep, they may experience fatigue, irritability, poor concentration, impaired judgment, reduced alertness, and increased risk of accidents and injuries. They may also develop or worsen mental health conditions such as depression, anxiety, post-traumatic stress disorder (PTSD), and substance abuse.

Therefore, improving sleep hygiene can have significant benefits for police officers' mental health. It can help them cope with stress, manage their emotions, improve their performance, and prevent or treat mental health problems. Sleep hygiene can also be part of a comprehensive wellness program that includes other strategies such as physical activity, healthy diet, social support, counseling, and mindfulness. By practicing good sleep hygiene, police officers can enhance their quality of life and protect their mental health.

Sleep is one of the essential building blocks of health; it is essential for all our biological processes, stable mental health and is when an incredible amount of repair in the body and brain occurs. If you aren't sleeping well, you are going to have a really hard time achieving your health goals. So, if you know that sleep isn't optimal, take the time to create healthy habits around it. Eat your last meal about 3 h before going to bed, have a warm shower about 1–2 h before sleep, turn off screens at least 2 h before going to sleep, go to sleep when you are tired, sleep in a dark and cool room, cut the alcohol, and try doing some gentle stretching or progressive muscle relaxing prior to sleep.

Connection

Sometimes this pillar is misconstrued as social connectedness. This pillar refers to your connection with yourself, with others (community), and the natural world around you.

Connection is a vital aspect of managing mental health, especially during challenging times. Connection refers to the sense of closeness and belonging that we feel when we interact with others who support and value us. Connection can help us cope with stress, improve our mood, and enhance our self-esteem. It can also provide us with a sense of purpose and meaning in life.

According to research, connection can have many benefits for our mental health, such as reducing symptoms of anxiety and depression, increasing resilience, and promoting trust.

Connection is not only important for managing mental health but also for enhancing our overall well-being and happiness. By connecting with others who share our values, interests, and goals, we can enrich our lives and make a positive difference in the world.

One of the ways I found useful was to connect with others who understood and supported you. Connection can foster a sense of belonging, trust, and safety, which are essential for recovery and resilience. Connection can also facilitate access to professional help when needed, as well as provide opportunities for learning and growth.

By fostering connection in managing police mental health, we can improve the outcomes of police interactions with people who have mental illness or are in crisis. We can also enhance the quality of life and well-being of police officers and their families.

A sense of belonging is key to our spiritual self. I often refer to law enforcement as a global family, one which I am immediately comfortable with despite jurisdictional difference, cultural and ethnic differences, or geographic difference. The trap was for me that over decades, my connectedness had narrowed to only those in the job. It is important that we develop relationships with a few important people who know you in combination with trust in your relationship with your own internal emotional landscape.

Yet, before I could expand my network, I had to develop a deep connection with myself to know what feels good about me, my body, my values, and what my heart really desired. I had to take stock of how I really wanted to live my life and with whom I wanted to spend my time with. Stress will continue forever if you are living out of alignment. But you need to know what your most aligned self looks like in order to follow that pathway to better mental health, well-being, and harmony.

Connection, too, is a practice. My journey continues in this space, and I am continuing to learn how I can better myself using therapy, other spiritual (not religious) guidance, meditation, writing, mindfulness, and breathing (to name but a few). We experience connection when we hug another human, practice gratitude, commit random acts of kindness, and put our bare feet on the earth or wade through the waters at the beach or just sitting in the sun and listening to the wind. Connection often requires a sense of intentionally slowing yourself down, which can be challenging at the current pace of life. So start small—assess your situation, establish a practice regime that suits your needs and desires, open your mind, and try a few different things to gauge what does and doesn't work for you.

Purpose/Identity

What is our true identity? How do we find our true purpose? Does a particular job, image, ethnicity, sexual orientation, temperament, or social status determine identity? For me, and many in policing, my identity is defined by my job. I had not really thought about my purpose and identity until after I was diagnosed with PTSD.

The truth is, purpose is what's most important to me in life. It's what drives me to get out of bed in the morning and follow through with the goals I've set for myself. It gives your life meaning and direction.

For me, purpose is intertwined with values. Determining my values was incredibly difficult to answer. To start, I asked myself, "What sort of person do I want to be?"

"What do I want to stand for?" and "What is meaningful to me?". To do so required me to reflect on my past. Reflecting on the past doesn't mean dwelling on things that have happened and view it as a representation of who you will always be! Rather, when we reflect on the past with a good balance of both logic and emotion, we can obtain information about ourselves that we may not have clearly known before and also embrace our past as a display of growth.

So, why is purpose and identity important in managing mental health?

Purpose and identity are two key aspects of our psychological well-being that help us to navigate the challenges and opportunities of life. Having a sense of purpose means having a stable and generalized intention to accomplish something that is meaningful to ourselves and of consequence to the world beyond ourselves. Having a sense of identity means having a clear and consistent understanding of who we are and how we fit into the world around us.

Both purpose and identity can have positive effects on our mental health. Research has shown that having a strong sense of purpose is associated with a lower risk of death, better physical health, and higher quality of life (Cohen et al., 2016). Having a healthy sense of identity leads to improved emotional regulation, self-esteem, and coping skills (Velotti, 2017). Purpose and identity can also motivate us to pursue our goals, overcome obstacles, and grow as individuals (Newman, 2020).

However, finding and maintaining purpose and identity can be challenging, especially in times of change, uncertainty, or crisis. We may struggle with existential questions such as "Who am I?" and "What do I want to do with my life?" We may feel disconnected from ourselves or others or experience a loss of meaning or direction. We may also face external pressures or expectations that conflict with our authentic selves.

Some strategies that have helped me include the following:

- Reflecting on my past experiences, relationships, achievements, and challenges and how they have shaped me
- Exploring my current interests, hobbies, talents, and passions and how they align with my personal values and goals
- Seeking out new opportunities for learning, growth, contribution, and connection that can enrich my life and expand my horizon
- Seeking feedback and support from others who share my vision or understand my struggles

By developing a strong sense of purpose and identity, we can enhance our mental health and well-being, as well as make a positive difference in the world.

I've since learned that the purpose is about finding and following your passions, nurturing what really enthuses you.

Conclusion

Being diagnosed with a mental illness like PTSD can be difficult. However, as I learned, a diagnosis would eventually become a relief, explaining why I was behaving and struggling like I was.

It took a lot of strength, but once I accepted my diagnosis and stopped blaming everything and everyone else for my position, only then could I truly begin the healing process.

The process of storytelling is not a substitute for professional treatments; rather, it is a complementary approach that can enhance the benefits of evidence-based therapies. It is not a onetime event that can magically erase the trauma or its effects. It is not a way to avoid facing the reality or the challenges of living with PTSI.

I indirectly learned that telling my lived experience story and the recovery processes has helped many. Conversely, I have learned so much from those who to have told the story of their lived experience and treatments.

Storytelling is a powerful way to cope with PTSI and to overcome the barriers that prevent people from seeking help. It can help police to heal their wounds, to connect with others who understand them, and to transform their pain into strength and wisdom. By sharing stories, they can not only improve their own mental health and well-being but also contribute to the social change and awareness that is needed to prevent and reduce stigma and elevate help-seeking behaviors in the policing profession.

Living with PTSI is tough, but it does not mean that police should feel alone and helpless or live in silence. There are many effective treatments for PTSI that can help a person recover from the trauma and regain a sense of control over their life. With the right mindset, alterations of lifestyle, commitment, treatment, and support, a person can heal from their trauma and live a fulfilling and meaningful life.

References

Adler, J. M., Lodi-Smith, J., Philippe, F. L., & Houle, I. (2016). The incremental validity of narrative identity in predicting well-being: A review of the field and recommendations for the future. *Personality and Social Psychology Review, 20*(2), 142–175. https://doi.org/10.1177/1088868315585068. Epub 2015 May 12.

Algorani, E. B., & Gupta, V. (2022). *Coping mechanisms*. StatPearls Publishing. PMID: 32644457.

Asalgoo, S., Gila, P., Meftahi, G., & Sahraei, H. (2016). Posttraumatic stress disorder (PTSD): Mechanisms and possible treatments. *Neurophysiology, 47*, 482–489. https://doi.org/10.1007/s11062-016-9559-9

Biro, M., Novović, Z., & Gavrilov, V. (1997). Coping strategies in PTSD. *Behavioural and Cognitive Psychotherapy, 25*(4), 365–369. https://doi.org/10.1017/S1352465800018762

Cohen, R., Bavishi, C., & Rozanski, A. (2016). Purpose in life and its relationship to all-cause mortality and cardiovascular events: A meta-analysis. *Psychosomatic Medicine, 78*(2), 122–133. https://doi.org/10.1097/PSY.0000000000000274

Dixon, S. (2021). Law enforcement suicide: The depth of the problem and best practices for suicide prevention strategies. *Aggression and Violent Behavior, 61*, 101649, ISSN 1359-1789. https://doi.org/10.1016/j.avb.2021.101649

Edwards, G. (2023). I'm not faking being sick, I'm faking being well: The need for leadership in mental health for policing. *Journal of Community Safety and Well-Being, 8*, S50–S56. https://doi.org/10.35502/jcswb.294

Gallagher, J. M. (2019). *The present of things past: An explorative case study of storytelling and sensemaking in policing*. ProQuest LLC, Ed.D. dissertation, Northeastern University. https://eric.ed.gov/?id=ED602124

Kamkar, K., Edwards, G., Hesketh, I., McFee, D., Papazoglou, K., Pedersen, P., Sanders, K., Stamatakis, T., & Thompson, J. (2020). Dialogue highlights from the LEPH2019 panel on police mental health and well-being. *Journal of Community Safety and Well-Being, 5*(1), 2–7. https://doi.org/10.35502/jcswb.123

Kurtz, D. L., Colburn, A., Fleetwood, J., Presser, L., Sandberg, S., & Ugelvik, T. (Eds.). (2019). *"Police narratives as allegories that shape police culture and behaviour". The Emerald handbook of narrative criminology* (pp. 321–341). Emerald Publishing Limited. https://doi.org/10.1108/978-1-78769-005-920191028

Lipov, E. (2023). *Survey reveals that renaming post-traumatic stress 'disorder' to 'injury' would reduce stigma*. Department of Surgery, University of Illinois Chicago. https://doi.org/10.7759/cureus.38888

Mitrousi, S., Travlos, A., Koukia, E., & Zyga, S. (2013). Theoretical approaches to coping. *International Journal of Caring Sciences, 6*, 131–137.

Newman, K. L. (2020). How purpose changes across your lifetime. *Greater Good Magazine. Science based insights for a meaningful life*. https://greatergood.berkeley.edu/

Papazoglou, K., & Tuttle, B. M. (2018). Fighting police trauma: Practical approaches to addressing psychological needs of officers. *SAGE Open, 8*(3). https://doi.org/10.1177/2158244018794794

Pitts, B. L., Eisenberg, M. L., Bailey, H. R., et al. (2022). PTSD is associated with impaired event processing and memory for everyday events. *Cognitive Research, 7*, 35. https://doi.org/10.1186/s41235-022-00386-6

Reiner, R., & Newburn, T. (2007). *Policing and the police*. 10.1093/he/9780199590278.003.0027

Renken, R. (2020). *How stories connect and persuade us: Unleashing the brain power of narrative*. https://www.npr.org/sections/health-shots/2020/04/11/815573198/how-stories-connect-and-persuade-us-unleashing-the-brain-power-of-narrative#:~:text=When%20you%20listen%20to%20a%20story%2C%20your%20brain,a%20person%27s%20motives%20and%20perspective%2C%20research%20has%20found

Rudofossi, D. (2009). *A cop doc's guide to public safety complex trauma syndrome: Using five police personality styles (death, value, and meaning)*. Baywood Publishing Company.

Rutledge, P. (2016). *Everything is story: Telling stories and positive psychology*. ABC-Clio.

Suzuki, W. A., Feliú-Mójer, M. I., Hasson, U., Yehuda, R., & Zarate, J. M. (2018). Dialogues: The science and power of storytelling. *The Journal of Neuroscience, 38*(44), 9468–9470. https://doi.org/10.1523/JNEUROSCI.1942-18.2018. PMID: 30381438; PMCID: PMC6209845.

US Department of Veterans Affairs. (2023). *PTSD: National Center for PTSD*. https://www.ptsd.va.gov/gethelp/selfhelp_coping.asp

Violanti, J. (2018). PTSD among police officers: Dispatch – Impact on critical decision making. *US DOJ COPS, 11*(5). https://cops.usdoj.gov/html/dispatch/05-2018/PTSD.html#:~:text=Police%20officers%20are%20often%20exposed%20to%20traumatic%20events%2C,their%20ability%20to%20perform%20duties%20to%20the%20public

Vogt, D. S., Shipherd, J. C., & Resick, P. A. (2012). Posttraumatic maladaptive beliefs scale: Evolution of the personal beliefs and reactions scale. *Assessment, 19*(3), 308–317. https://doi.org/10.1177/1073191110376161

Wagner, S. L., White, N., Fyfe, T., Matthews, L. R., Randall, C., Regehr, C., White, M., Alden, L. E., Buys, N., Carey, M. G., Corneil, W., Fraess-Phillips, A., Krutop, E., & Fleischmann, M. H. (2020). Systematic review of posttraumatic stress disorder in police officers following routine work-related critical incident exposure. *American Journal of Industrial Medicine, 63*(7), 600–615. https://doi.org/10.1002/ajim.23120. Epub 2020 May 17. PMID: 32419181.

Wallace, D., Jallat, E., & Jetly, R. (2020). Post-traumatic stress disorder or post-traumatic stress injury: What's in a name? *Journal of Military and Veterans Health, 28*(1), 39–44. https://search.informit.org/doi/10.3316/informit.079805034525323

A Biopsychosocial Approach to Officer Wellness

Katrina Sanders

Law enforcement operations are underpinned by evidence and so are approaches to patient care, health and ill-health, and include the practical application of the findings of the best available research. Evidence-based approaches to preventing ill-health in law enforcement officers do not differ significantly from the communities in which they serve, and this is foundational when designing workplace health prevention strategies. Too often the strategies focus narrowly on mental health, with somewhat disregard of other key contributing adjuncts to health such as leadership, organizational culture, the physical stress of load carry and use of force, and fatigue, among others. This chapter explores evidence-based approaches to protecting mental health in law enforcement officers.

Commissioners, leaders, policymakers, and practitioners regularly ask me "what works?". The inference is that the medical community has the answer or is a one-stop shop for health prevention and intervention activities. Of course, the reality is that like human health, organizational health and the protection of health in law enforcement officers are a complex interplay of a number of systems.

The Individual
A biopsychosocial model of health recognizes biological, psychological, and social systems can all impact individual health.

The biopsychosocial model of care (Francesc Borrell-Carrio, 2004) provides a framework to understand the multidimensional aspects of suffering, disease, and illness, with environmental context. The model requires deep understanding of the context the patient is living and working in and respects that nontraditional medical

K. Sanders (✉)
Australian Federal Police, Canberra, ACT, Australia

K. Papazoglou, K. Kamkar (eds.), *Multi-faceted Approaches to Challenges and Coping in Law Enforcement*, https://doi.org/10.1007/978-3-031-62825-2_2

inputs can equally affect individual health. In this model, the case example of hypertension (elevated blood pressure) is not only treated with blood pressure lowering medication but also with lifestyle prescription including (but not limited to) stress reduction strategies, sleep hygiene, alcohol reduction strategies, nutrition, and exercise interventions. Now take the biopsychosocial approach for every individual within a police agency, aggregate that approach at a population level, and add environmental factors—the result is a framework to support health and well-being for the entire workforce.

The Organization
A holistic model of health recognizes physical, psychological, social, and organizational systems all impact individual and therefore population health (David Kindig, 2003).

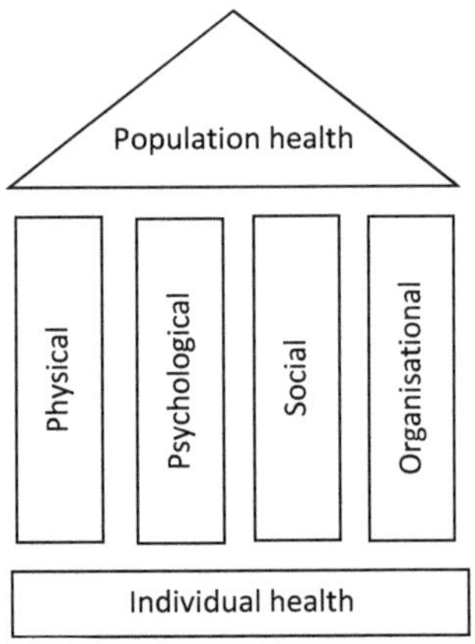

Holistic approach to health and well-being in law enforcement jurisdictions

Four pillars—physical, psychological, social, organizational—form the foundation of health and well-being strategies for law enforcement jurisdictions. Health and well-being are a complex interplay of these pillars at an individual, role, team, operational, and organizational level (population health). This approach connects the tactical level inputs of individuals, roles, and operations, to strategic level capability and ultimately the achievement of business objectives. If the on-the-ground inputs are not functioning (i.e., biopsychosocial approach is not harnessed) or are unequally weighted in one pillar (such as psychological health emphasized as more important than physical health), then organizational capability is eroded.

Case Study 1: Physical Injury

A 43-year-old police officer with lower back pain due to years of load carry seeks support for early intervention and physiotherapy—workplace is unwilling to support time away from work for treatment or financial support. Over time, the lower back injury worsens, and the officer is unable to undertake his duties and takes an extended period of sick leave. During this time, the officer becomes isolated from work colleagues, engages in unhealthy self-coping strategies (increased alcohol consumption), and develops a secondary psychological injury.

Intervention

Early treatment and support to recover from physical injury may have prevented the psychological injury.

Case Study 2: Organizational Red Tape

An officer has applied for a specialist role, a lifelong dream. The application process takes close to 6 months and involves written application, referee check, and medical and psychological evaluation, among other gateways. The officer has postponed the psychological evaluation on three occasions as the supervisor will not support release from duty to attend the evaluation. Subsequently, the application is denied due to failure of meeting all gateway requirements. The officer feels anger and resentment toward the organization—he is diagnosed with adjustment disorder and requires time away from the workplace to recover.

Intervention

Organizational policy and systems that support the officer to attend gateway evaluations.

Equal investment in physical, psychological, social, and organizational health pillars supports the biopsychosocial model of care for individuals and a holistic approach to health and well-being in law enforcement jurisdictions. Policing is a high-risk occupation with a high risk of injury—physical, psychological, and social. Physical health threats include musculoskeletal injury, high rates of hypertension (elevated blood pressure), high cholesterol, sleep disorders, and ultimately cardiovascular disease. Psychological risks in law enforcement are well-known and often exacerbated by organizational health threats such as red tape, favoritism, lack of resources, and inability to spend time with friends and family (such as regular shift changes). Ultimately the police officer's social health suffers either through relationship breakdown, isolation from usual activities and groups, or self-destructive behavior such as gambling, increased alcohol intake, or other high-risk activities.

The biopsychosocial model of care is grounded in evidence; the practitioner and patient must strive for good health in each of the biological, psychological, and social pillars, equally. Overinvestment in one pillar risks underinvestment in another. The tactical response officer, undertaking intense daily physical training, conducting high pressure operations, must equally invest in psychological and social health. The officer participating in regular psychological screening must equally invest in physical training to prevent injury. This model can easily be applied at an organizational level, or population health level, by aggregating the individual level interventions to a population level with equal investment. Leaders, policymakers, and health practitioners can use this holistic model as a framework to approach health prevention, promotion, and protection, within their organization.

Health Risk Assessment

A simple "health risk assessment" is the first step in understanding the health risks within the agency and therefore the potential holistic mitigation strategies. Health risk assessments are not designed to be overly burdensome; they can be completed in a timely and efficient method. Evaluating data can be the most resource-intensive component; however, it is the most important component of the assessment—without an understanding of the data, the "problem" remains undefined.

Current State

1. Evaluate available data such as incident data, workers' compensation claims, professional standards, human resource data (such as complaints and absenteeism data).
2. Seek verbatim feedback through interviews, surveys, and focus groups.
3. Include external stakeholders to build a picture of risk including associations, unions, family groups, retired members.
4. Consider what *is* working.
5. Review relevant human resource policies—do they reflect a culture where recovery from injury is presumed?
6. Evaluate senior leader and broader organization readiness for change.

Gap Analysis

1. Review the current state from a patient-centric approach—how would the police officer view the current state? Does the current state deliver a biopsychosocial approach to individual health? Where are the gaps?
2. Now review the current state from an organizational level (population health level)—is there a holistic model of health? Consider leadership commitment and

understanding, and review human resource frameworks and appropriate resources in the right areas—are critical transition points identified and well supported (such as international deployment or transition to retirement)? Where are the gaps from an organizational approach?

Strategy

1. Prioritize the gaps by risk (high, medium, low) and by resource investment (high, medium, low).
2. Create a strategy to reduce the gaps. The strategy should be practical, achievable, and measurable, with appropriate governance (such as a steering committee or board).
3. Understand how progress will be measured. Map this progress against the information obtained in the current state.

Evidence-Based Interventions

The choice of intervention or program within each pillar should be evidence-based, culturally appropriate (what works for one agency will not necessarily work for another), accepted by the workforce, supported by systems and policy, and championed by leadership. With so many offerings in the health and well-being arena, it is challenging to know which are evidence-based and where to invest finite resources.

Physical

1. Physical training programs targeted at individuals and teams
2. Early intervention program for treatment of acute physical injuries
3. Screening programs for cardiovascular disease, hearing, sleep disorders, and relevant occupational exposures (such as asbestos or tuberculosis screening)
4. Vaccination programs
5. Nutrition education

Psychological

1. Robust pre-entry psychological screening
2. Ongoing psychological screening
3. Stigma reducing campaigns
4. Specific training for leaders and supervisors
5. Peer support program
6. Stepped care approach to mental health support and intervention

Organizational

1. Health education program (aimed at preventing illness)
2. Workers' compensation training for leaders
3. Preparation for separation or retirement
4. Developing reporting tools to assist managers understand health risk profile

5. Returning to work policies

Social

1. Rosters that support the worker and the family
2. Encouraging support networks for officers and families, especially those created by officers and families
3. Retired member groups

These programs should be available from "cradle to grave," for the life of the law enforcement officer. Early career education on the importance of health prevention activities, and early career encouragement and support to participate in health prevention activities, creates a culture where health is valued. In turn, this culture provides a safe environment where ill-health can be reported and supported, free from prejudice and punishment. The impact of workplace culture on health is significant; thriving supportive cultures foster an environment where help and recovery from ill-health are presumed—the opposite workplace culture is one where ill-health is shrouded in secrecy and where individuals are presumed malingering and punished.

Irrespective of the strategies employed, either in their infancy or exceedingly mature, strategies are not "set and forget." A regular review and evaluation process (Glasgow, 2019) are required to ensure the strategy is contemporary, fit-for-purpose, and consistent with agency objectives:

A holistic approach, or holistic strategy, to the prevention of mental ill-health in law enforcement is grounded in evidence. Policymakers, leaders, and mental health professionals have for too long neglected the biopsychosocial model of healthcare to the detriment of the law enforcement officer and, more broadly, the agency. A shift away from "mental health" and toward "well-being" encapsulates the biopsychosocial model and adopts a multifaceted approach to preventing ill-health. Law enforcement agencies need to understand their own well-being needs, adopt holistic strategies to support these needs, and embrace a culture of evaluation and continuous improvement that ultimately protects the health of officers.

References

David Kindig, G. S. (2003). What is population health? *American Journal of Public Health, 93*(3), 380–383.

Francesc Borrell-Carrio, A. L. (2004). The biopsychosocial model 25 years later: Principles, practice, and scientific inquiry. *Annals of Family Medicine, 2*(6), 576–582.

Glasgow, H. G. (2019). *RE-AIM planning and evaluation framework: Adapting to new science and practice with a 20-year review* (Vol. 7, p. 64). Frontiers in Public Health.

Revolutionizing Mental Health in Policing Through Resiliency and Transformational Leadership

Thomas Carrique

Our People: A Healthy and Resilient OPP

I truly believe that the most important mission as Commissioner of the Ontario Provincial Police (OPP), and the most important responsibility of any police leader, is to look after our people. It is the primary responsibility of any leader to ensure that they take care of and support those who they are entrusted to lead. We have a collective responsibility to look out for each other's well-being. The days of not having the courage to talk about health issues, to accept and show vulnerability, and to address the underlying issues are over. We can no longer accept that mental health does not affect our workplace, communities, and society.

Mental health is a topic that is extremely important to me, both on a personal and professional level. I believe that by sharing our experiences, we can encourage understanding, empathy, and support for one another. Through my own journey, I have come to realize the profound impact that mental health can have on every aspect of our lives. We simply cannot ignore it or brush it aside. Mental and physical health are intimately intertwined and cannot be separated. Mental health *is* health.

I have gained greater insight through the courage of others who have shared their experiences freely and in the aftermath of suicide of colleagues and a close family friend. It allowed me to develop empathy, resilience, and a deep appreciation for the importance of mental health. My experiences fueled my passion to become an advocate, to raise awareness about mental health, and to encourage others to seek support.

T. Carrique (✉)
Ontario Provincial Police, Orillia, ON, Canada
e-mail: thomas.carrique@opp.ca

K. Papazoglou, K. Kamkar (eds.), *Multi-faceted Approaches to Challenges and Coping in Law Enforcement*, https://doi.org/10.1007/978-3-031-62825-2_3

Suicide Deaths of Our Officers

When I assumed the role of Commissioner of the OPP in April of 2019, the organization was in the midst of coping with the grief and loss of suicide deaths of three of its members within a 3-week period in the summer of 2018. These tragic deaths brought the topic of mental health into organizational discourse and prompted the OPP to launch a multifaceted internal review of ways it could better support members by examining its policies, programs, and practices relating to the well-being of its members.

It is important to note that suicide deaths of workers are not unique to the OPP—it is a global issue that has garnered worldwide attention. According to a report by the Mental Health Commission of Canada (2018), suicide ranks among the top 10 leading causes of death in the country, and a substantial proportion of individuals who died by suicide were grappling with mental health challenges.

Police suicide in Canada is a concerning and complex issue that has drawn significant attention from researchers and experts. The tragic phenomenon of police officers dying by suicide underscores the urgent need for better understanding and support within law enforcement agencies. While it is unclear at this time whether suicide rates among police officers are higher related to the general population, studies have indicated elevated rates of mental health difficulties within the police service. Recent Canadian research has established a distressing pattern, revealing higher prevalence rates of mental health symptoms among police personnel than in the general public, with factors such as exposure to traumatic events and the quality of interpersonal relationships playing crucial roles (Carleton et al., 2017, 2018). The toll of untreated mental health injuries on police officers can be profound, impacting their overall well-being, cognitive abilities, and job performance, with potential ripple effects on organizational efficiency (Elovainio et al., 2000). These insights emphasize the critical importance of fostering a comprehensive support system that addresses the unique challenges faced by police officers, ultimately contributing to their mental health and overall quality of life.

Experiencing negative mental health states can also affect general cognitive and physical skills and abilities. In fact, first responders who report elevated symptoms of post-traumatic stress disorder (PTSD) have shown significant performance deficits when completing complex cognitive tasks, including assessing risks, planning multistep responses to an emergency, and paying attention to competing stimuli. These are all critical skills for police officers both from a public safety and personal safety perspective.[1] Other researchers have found that first responders with PTSD symptoms were more likely to be injured on the job.[2] In addition to improved officer

[1] Regehr, C. & LeBlanc, V. (2017) PTSD, Acute Stress, Performance and Decision-Making in Emergency Service Workers. Journal of the American Academy of Psychiatry and the Law, 45, 184–192

[2] Katsavouni, F., Bebetsos, E., Malliou, P., & Beneka, A. (2016). The relationship between burnout, PTSD symptoms and injuries in firefighters. *Occupational Medicine, 66,* 32–37. Retrieved from

safety, protecting police well-being can result in increased productivity and organizational efficiency. In fact, failure to address vicarious or direct trauma or recognize workplace challenges can result in: (1) lost productivity (e.g., decreased morale, cohesion, communication, collaboration, and quality of services), (2) staff turnover (e.g., lost time and resources needed to hire and train new staff which drains the remaining staff), and (3) poor organization health (e.g., erosion of concentration, focus, decision-making, motivation, and performance).[3]

The organizational impact of a police suicide can be profound. The suicide of a colleague has multifold effects on the organization, and its effects may be felt over time. A suicide within the police service can lead to a significant decrease in morale and team cohesion and anger with the organization. Colleagues may feel a sense of loss or guilt and even blame themselves for not recognizing the signs, which can affect teamwork and camaraderie. The suicide of a fellow police member can exacerbate the stigma surrounding mental health issues in law enforcement. Police service members may be hesitant to seek help for their own mental health issues due to fear of judgment, perceived impact on career, or feelings of guilt for creating additional work for colleagues if they go on leave. The emotional toll of coping with the loss can lead to emotional exhaustion and reduced job satisfaction. The handling of a suicide within the organization can also affect its reputation. If officers perceive that the department is not providing adequate support or taking proactive support measures, it could reflect poorly on the department's leadership. Leadership within the organization might face challenges in addressing the incident appropriately while maintaining operations. Balancing the needs of the officers, maintaining organizational stability, and handling public relations can be complex. To mitigate these effects, law enforcement agencies should prioritize mental health support, provide resources for officers, offer grief counseling, promote open discussions about mental health, and implement suicide prevention programs. Addressing these issues proactively can help minimize the negative impact of a police suicide on the organization and its members.

A Look Back

In 2012, the Ontario Ombudsman, André Marin, undertook an extensive review of how the OPP and the Ministry of Community Safety and Correctional Services (MCSCS) were addressing operational stress injuries (OSIs) among police officers and correctional officers. The term "operational stress injuries (OSIs)" refers to any mental health condition resulting from operational stressors while serving in a

https://academic.oup.com/occmed/article/66/1/32/2750638

[3] Kalergis, K.I., & Molnar, B.E. (2017). NCVRW Creating a Vicarious Trauma-Informed Organization: Strategies for Success [Webinar]. Retrieved from https://ovc.ncjrs.gov/pdftxt/Creating_a_Vicarious_Trauma-Informed_Organization_Strategies_for_Success_Recording_Presentation_508.pdf

professional capacity, especially in military or other public safety professions (Canadian Institute for Public Safety Research and Treatment, 2019). The review entitled *In the Line of Duty* reported a total of 23 OPP officer suicides from 1989 to 2012 as compared with 21 other on-duty deaths. The Ombudsman report included 28 recommendations to the OPP. In an effort to address the recommendations of the Ombudsman, the OPP introduced a number of new programs between 2012 and 2015 with a goal of improving the health and well-being of its members.

The OPP's Wellness Unit was officially formed in 2014 and included the expansion of the peer support program and appointment of a centralized, full-time Provincial Peer Support Coordinator. Significant efforts were made to reduce stigma and encourage conversations on mental health through initiatives such as supervisor training on managing for a healthy workplace, and all employees received the Mental Health Commission of Canada (MHCC) adaptation of the Department of National Defence (DND)'s Road to Mental Readiness (R2MR) training. Fitness and lifestyle programs were introduced, and the existing volunteer Chaplaincy program was expanded. However, while employees now had improved and direct support from various sources, the legacy of the three suicides in 2018 continued to reverberate, and more work was clearly required to address the challenges that members face.

The Reviews

In August 2018, the OPP launched an internal review into the suicide deaths of OPP officers as well as a series of mental health roundtables with members and families. At the same time, two external reviews were being launched independently of one another. The Ministry of the Solicitor General which oversees the OPP commissioned an independent review of the workplace culture of the OPP, and the Office of the Chief Coroner in Ontario established an expert panel to examine the conditions underlying police officer suicides in Ontario.

Breaking the Silence

Recognizing the stigma associated with mental health, it was critical to ensure we worked with our members and their families to break down the barriers that may have contributed to members seeking support. A critical component of the internal reviews centered on the OPP Mental Health Review, which was directed by then Commissioner Vince Hawkes led by two Chief Superintendents and included OPP members, family members, and external stakeholders and experts.

The first stage involved meeting with current and retired OPP members who were willing to speak about their experiences. The Chief Superintendents traveled to all OPP regions across the province to conduct comprehensive consultations in different formats and settings, including one-on-one conversations, forums, and roundtables. In the second stage of the roundtable review, the two Chief Superintendents engaged with impacted family members to seek their perspectives and to better understand their experiences and any difficulties they had in supporting their loved ones. The final stage was a consultation with external stakeholders, researchers, and experts with field experience in assisting first responders in crisis.

The feedback and perspective provided by each of these groups was essential to help build and further inform on how to better support members and their families from a mental health standpoint.

In an effort to identify and examine barriers that prevented OPP members from seeking assistance and support for issues related to mental health, the OPP offered voluntary participation in roundtable discussions held from November 2018 to May 2019. Participants were offered the option to participate in small groups or private individual sessions. Sessions lasted 2 h on average. Participants included active civilian and uniform members, retired members, families of OPP officers who died by suicide, families of OPP members, internal support services, other police agencies, contracted service providers, the three OPP associations (representing all levels of rank, uniformed and civilian), third-party providers, and managers and supervisors. Approximately 465 consultations were conducted, the majority of which were with OPP employees.

The report developed from the roundtable discussions was divided into three separate categories: proactive mental health, intervention, and recovery. Additionally, the report identified three distinct stressors, one or all of which can result from direct or indirect exposure to calls for service: organizational, operational, and personal. The report highlighted the keen need for an extensive network of supports readily and easily accessible to active, retired, and family members in perpetuity. Based on the consultations that occurred, a significant number of recommendations were developed that aimed at encouraging change to existing practices throughout the continuum of a member's career, from recruit through to retirement, and for their families as key supports to our membership. The release of the OPP's findings from the Mental Health Review and other internal reviews was preceded by a joint announcement made in March 2019, with the Ontario government providing funding to the Ontario Provincial Police Association (OPPA) for the development and administration of a comprehensive mental health program for all active and retired OPPA members.

Roundtable discussions identified that, while the Employee Family Assistance Program (EFAP) provided a number of helpful services to members, service providers lacked the specialized training and experience necessary to support first responders with operational stress injuries. As a result, the creation of a specialized clinical services department was recommended to bridge this gap. In addition, many recommendations included a strong focus on education and training to reduce stigma, encourage self-help, and open lines of communication related to mental health issues.

Independent Review Panel (IRP) Report on OPP Workplace Culture: External Review

Concurrent with the OPP's internal reviews, the Ministry of the Solicitor General commissioned an independent panel to review the OPP's workplace culture. The independent panel conducted a survey of OPP members (over 5000 responses received), held roundtable discussions with 55 members, and held one-on-one interviews with another 18 members as well as with 4 family members of OPP members who died by suicide. The result was the Ontario Provincial Police Independent Review Panel: Final Report (2019) in which the panel made the following observations and recommendations:

Leadership and organizational responsibility for wellness and positive workplace culture is required [Recommendations 1 and 2]. In addition to the important work already done with the internal OPP reviews and externally in the policing community, the Commissioner and his command team must have direct access to and dialog with the diverse voices, expertise, and lived experience of members, mental health clinicians, family members, and other critical stakeholders across all regions and bureaus. A holistic approach to wellness—bringing the biological, psychological, social, and spiritual elements of health together—must be combined with organizational restructuring to support the Commissioner's mandate. A dedicated healthy workplace bureau with expertise, regional presence, and appropriate resourcing would allow for greater coordination in support services, regional access to programming, and ongoing analysis of the challenges related to well-being in policing.

Leadership is a critical element in workplace culture [Recommendations 3 and 4]. A healthy and resilient workplace requires effective and engaged leadership, at every level of the organization. Members shared many experiences, positive and negative, of the impact of leaders on their well-being and that of their colleagues. In the survey, leadership was cited as a top recommendation for improvement to the workplace culture of the OPP. The traditional model of police leadership—top-down/paramilitary—would require innovation and culture change to better respond to the crisis in well-being. Leadership must support a climate of well-being, a positive team environment where leader role modeling validates early help-seeking behavior and support becomes a shared function with team members also looking out for one another. The panel heard repeated, vehement skepticism with respect to both real and perceived bias of the OPP's promotional process and about common incidents of nepotism and cronyism in management hiring.

The Panel strongly endorsed efforts to improve transparency and accountability in the promotions process, including the participation of a neutral manager in the hiring process, the alignment of the process, and the definition of merit with the organizational expectations of leadership and more rigorous use of tools such as the existing talent pools.

Mental health services should be accessible and credible [Recommendations 5–10]. The OPP's response to members in crisis has a significant impact on the likelihood of improvement. In other words, how the organization responds to individuals—through the credibility and expertise of services and through the support or stigmatization by peers and supervisors—can either help or further exacerbate trauma, the latter of which can lead to a sense of betrayal by the organization. The panel encouraged the OPP to evaluate its current services and programs; to consider opportunities to develop a common language around mental health, wellness, and resilience among members; and to immediately provide resources to members and supervisors to assist them in navigating the complex array of options and obligations members face when seeking mental health supports.

Positive workplace culture requires trusted oversight and dialog [Recommendations 11–13]. Ongoing dialog, discussions using a common and strengths-based language across the organization, the practice of conflict resolution, and modeling of constructive approaches at all levels of leadership are necessary to communicate expectations to members. It was recommended that an organizational restructuring occur that would create a separate unit for workplace conflict resolution which would have responsibility for the "repatriation" of the Respectful Workplace Policy, adapting it to better suit the context and desired outcomes.

The administration of the operation and its people should support wellness and positive workplace culture [Recommendations 14 and 15]. Across the province, the panel heard about stressors including staffing shortages, long shifts, challenging shift cycles, and pressures related to working overtime, which were taking their toll on members. At the time of the IRP report, about 875 or 21% of frontline members were off on an approved leave, including sick leave, parental leave, and other forms of authorized absence. This is a high cost to taxpayers, to public safety, and to the wellness of members continuing to work. It was recommended that staffing decisions be made to ensure adequate time for rest and recovery between challenging shifts and after critical incidents and with a view to reducing the isolation of members at work. There are areas of the province and specific detachments and units where the staffing levels are so low as to be considered a crisis. The panel encouraged the OPP and the provincial government to pay specific and immediate attention to staffing in northern Ontario with a view to increasing the number of northern-based members and the available supports to members in northern detachments (parts of northern Ontario are remote and widespread with much of it comprised of Indigenous communities that are particularly isolated as fly-in communities. OPP members deployed in the northern Ontario have limited access to all kinds of resources and spend long periods of time away from family). Staffing in the OPP does not currently reflect the diverse nature of Ontario's population in terms of gender, ethnicity, or identity. The IRP report stated that diversity in staffing and meaningful inclusion inside the organization are critical elements of a healthy workplace. The leadership team was encouraged to lead a collaborative campaign to increase efforts to strengthen diverse groups of members.

Our Members Spoke: We Listened

The internal and external reviews conducted provided the OPP with an opportunity to learn from the tragedies and struggles of its membership and, in some cases, their families as well.

I wish to thank the members and their families who had the strength and courage to come forward and share their experiences and participate in the process, who allowed themselves to be vulnerable and to put sometimes complex and negative feelings aside in their quests to help other OPP members and their families. Additionally, I would like to acknowledge each of the project leads and their respective teams for the tremendous work to complete the reviews. I attribute a great deal of credit to all the OPP members who led and assisted with the internal reviews and the leadership of the Ontario Provincial Police Association's commitment to the well-being of our members. It took an enormous amount of physical and emotional effort to ensure we evolve our programming and provide the supports necessary for our members.

In July and August of 2019, a team and I traveled across Ontario hosting sessions in the various regions to discuss the findings of the OPP Mental Health Review and other internal reviews and to listen to what members and their families had to say.

I was saddened by the pain and suffering so many had experienced. It took tremendous strength and courage by the members who shared their stories and offered suggestions for change. It was during the follow-up conversations I had with our members when it dawned on me that the most important thing we need to do is to get our members comfortable talking about mental health. Police officers suffer the same illnesses or injuries as anyone else. Whether it be a medical condition or physical injury or a mental health illness, we are human beings requiring appropriate treatment, support, or resources regardless of the condition.

Policing takes courage. It is the bravest of the brave who risk their lives and health every day to protect our communities, something they do almost effortlessly—but it takes more courage to come forward and ask for help when we are suffering psychologically. Our police members are regularly exposed to the horrors of human depravity, and they and their families make many sacrifices throughout a policing career for the safety of their communities. Increased risk of injury is inherent in professions demanding high performance on a regular basis. Just as we would expect professional athletes to experience some injuries throughout their careers, so too can we expect police officers and civilians exposed to potentially traumatic events to experience physical or psychological operational stress injuries throughout their public safety careers. Addressed with appropriate support early and ensuring they remain "part of the team" throughout recovery, the risks of OSIs worsening into long-term mental health disorders can be mitigated.

From recruitment into retirement, proactive strategies to support member coping and resilience must remain forefront, evolving to meet member needs. The implementation of a range of supports, offered at multiple entry level points from prevention to early intervention to crisis, is crucial to assisting members. Respecting the individual's right to health privacy and assigning or identifying resources to support a member through a health issue are not unreasonable expectations. Members' families are essential supports to maintaining a healthy workforce. Access to programs and services should be enhanced to reflect the role of the family in ensuring member mental health and well-being.

Revolutionizing Mental Health in Policing

I arrived in the OPP as the internal reviews were being concluded and prior to the external review commencing. One of my first priorities was to oversee the completion of the recommendations associated to the reviews and the implementation of these recommendations, which focused on improving members' access to mental health supports while at the same time transforming the organizational culture. This was a very tall order, requiring the unwavering support of the existing leadership team, the OPPA Executive, Wounded Warriors Canada, Badge of Life Canada, Boots on the Ground, and Canada Beyond the Blue, particularly arriving as a newcomer in a large provincial organization of approximately 9600 members and auxiliary officers spread across over 1 million square kilometers, but one we were collectively determined to address. We owe it to all our members—officers, civilians, retirees, and auxiliaries—to get it right and reduce the fears and anxiety about coming forward and asking for help.

It was time to put the recommendations into *action* and important that we make the right changes. Some changes could be implemented quickly, while others require additional staffing resources, funding, or training.

The 2020–2022 OPP Healthy Workplace Strategy and Action Plan After a year in the making, the Healthy Workplace Strategy and Action Plan was launched as the OPP's action plan moving forward. The strategy takes into consideration the recommendations from the internal and external reviews and is a result of the collective and active participation, engagement, and consultations from across the province. The strategy envisions a healthy, safe, and inclusive workplace where members are supported in achieving their potential. The recommendations from the internal and external reviews are grouped under five key objectives. The objectives are listed below, followed by an overview of the actions underway.

The strategy included the following five objectives:

1. *Culture Change*
   Building trust, a sense of responsibility, and capability at all levels to create a culture in which members' psychological health and well-being are supported and protected
2. *Enhanced Access to Services*
   Ensuring timely access to quality, professional mental health programs, and services for members and their families

3. *Support Through Transitions*
   Supporting our members and their families from recruitment through retirement and all transitions in between
4. *Supportive Policies and Processes*
   Reducing risks to members' psychological health through the introduction of supportive policies and processes
5. *Mental Health Literacy*
   Reducing stigma and creating an environment where coworkers and supervisors are supportive of employees' psychological and mental health concerns and respond appropriately as needed

It is important that the entire organization cooperates fully to ensure that psychological health, safety, and respect are integrated into every facet of its operations. Responsibility for health and well-being must become entrenched in every aspect of the way the organization operates and engages with its members. While exposure to potentially traumatic incidents cannot be prevented, what can be changed are organizational processes and practices. Research has been increasingly showing that organizational stressors (e.g., policies, workload, supervisor interactions) have at least as much, if not more, impact on members' health and wellness (Carleton et al., 2020; Queirós et al., 2020). The OPP is continuously working to coordinate the delivery of the five objectives within the organization.

Culture Change OPP members who had experienced physical or mental health injuries or illnesses spoke about the importance of management and colleagues being understanding and supportive of them; the harm caused by judgmental comments and attitudes toward them; how they felt betrayed by the organization when no one reached out to them while they were off work; how some of the programs and processes in place to assist members who are struggling actually perpetuate their pain; the difficulties they faced coming forward for help as a result of personal and/or organizational stigma; and the guilt they felt when they did take time off due to the resulting increase in workload for their colleagues.

What We Are Doing The Healthy Workplace Strategy also recognizes, perhaps most importantly, that in order to successfully achieve a healthy, safe, and inclusive workplace, transformational culture change is required. Strong leadership, consistent action, and time will be required before such change achieves meaningful traction in the organization.

Culture change and evolution start with strong leadership. Leadership demands responsibility: the responsibility to do the right thing for the right reason every time, especially for a police leader who is accountable for leading the brave women and men who commit themselves and risk their lives to protect the public from harm and to safeguard the quality of life in our communities. It is not paradoxical to state that strong leadership also requires vulnerability: vulnerability to acknowledge that we cannot know everything all the time and that we must take the time and interest to learn from the past and be willing to take responsibility for and engage in the present. We have the ability and responsibility to learn from the past to create a better future.

I am interested in people-centered leaders who want to be coaches and mentors, who want to develop our members into leaders, and through that development who want to propel the overall performance of our organization into the highest level of excellence. To do that, it is crucial to be people-centered in all decision-making and consider our people's needs. That is why we made significant changes to the promotional process starting with the senior command levels to include a "360 evaluation" in which feedback is collected from all levels of the organization within their command.

I expect from our leaders that they always act with the OPP values in mind—that they

- Serve with pride, professionalism, and honor.
- Interact with respect, compassion, and fairness.
- Lead with integrity, honesty, and courage.

These values need to be demonstrated by our leadership and embedded in our processes and practices in our day-to-day work and interactions. Together, with the Commissioner's Command Team, I introduced an agreement that was based on these values and the principles of leadership. The agreement is signed by each one of the successful candidates as part of the promotional process to the highest levels of command as an affirmation of their commitment. The OPP has also developed leadership training with a people-centered approach being delivered to all levels of command and supervisors and specific training on organizational stressors, and we are launching the new promotional process for the remaining ranks that will include the same components.

In September 2020, the Office of Professionalism, Respect, Inclusion and Leadership (OPRIL) was established to ensure that the OPP values are embedded in everyday actions and interactions. OPRIL's mandate is to influence organizational leadership and workplace culture to ensure that our OPP values are integrated in all of our policies, procedures, practices, and most importantly actions.

More recently, the new Culture and Strategy Services Command was created in 2023 with the responsibility for key transformational change within the OPP, to allow for greater capacity, better collaboration across provincial commands, and improved accountability to address key organizational functions. The command is well positioned to help drive workplace culture enhancements, consistent with the OPP's Strategic Plan, Anti-racism Action Plan, and Anti-sexual Harassment Action Plan, and ensure recommendations from the various reviews and reports are successfully implemented.

Enhanced Access to Services OPP members cited concerns about the lack of access to professional help from clinicians who understand policing and have experience treating OSIs. Concerns were also raised about the confidentiality of services provided through the OPP and members objected to having to contact peer support in order to access the OPP's Community Referral List (a list of vetted clinicians in communities throughout the province).

Family members reported challenges accessing information about OPP services and supports and difficulty getting help for their loved ones. Members require timely access to quality mental health services delivered by professionals who understand policing and are experienced in treating OSIs.

What We Are Doing One of the first initiatives was to establish a new bureau, the OPP Healthy Workplace Team (HWT), that underlines the commitment of the organization to the health of its members, families, retirees, and auxiliary members. The Healthy Workplace Team provides access to a wide range of health and wellness services and is comprised of psychologists, mental health clinicians, and care navigators. The team also offers fitness and nutrition services. The Healthy Workplace Team coordinates organizational and wellness programs including peer support and the police chaplains. The Team also coordinates and supports the occupational medicine program for employees and managers which is delivered by an external occupational physician with expertise in occupational medicine and disability management. The HWT has begun an operational reintegration support program that oversees in-service trainers work with members soon after a potentially traumatic incident and with members returning to work after a medical leave to help gradually reintegrate back into the work environment. Taken together, the reintegration program and occupational medicine program help members to remain at work and successfully return to work after a leave.

Historically, the accommodation or return-to-work for employees with an illness, injury, or disability has sometimes been difficult, as identified in the 2019 Independent Review Panel report and OPP Mental Health Review. The OPP changed the way we do business with the establishment of an occupational medicine program to assist with removal and management of medical information outside of the organization as part of the injury/illness/return-to-work and stay-at-work process.

Occupational medicine is a medical specialty that focuses on the employer and employees' interactions with medical and occupational issues. The Royal College of Physicians and Surgeons of Canada[4] identifies it as the discipline that deals with the health needs of workers with respect to their working environments.

The OPP has procured the services of external occupational health professionals to provide expert opinion on medical documentation that is required to facilitate employee injury, illness, and accommodation while respecting employees' rights to privacy regarding personal health issues.

Whereas previously, members' personal medical documentation was submitted to an employee's manager, the organization can now protect member medical privacy by removing personal health information from the organization. Medical documentation is instead routed through an occupational medicine team for review, and only the occupationally relevant information (i.e., restrictions and limitations) is

[4] https://www.omsoc.org/The-Occupational-Specialist-An-Overview

communicated to the manager and the employee. Managers no longer collect medical notes and will direct employees to submit their documentation to the occupational physician instead of anyone in the OPP. This is an opportunity for employees to have their medical information reviewed and refined by a medical specialist to ensure that the information being delivered to their employer respects their privacy and addresses only work-specific issues. Clarity and open, honest, respectful conversations are pivotal; building trusting relationships is a key foundation of the return-to-work or remain-at-work accommodation processes. If the employee and manager together decide further information would be beneficial as part of the process, they can reach out to the occupational doctor for further assistance with medical information.

To offer further access to services, support, and resources, the OPP also established partnerships with external service providers Badge of Life Canada, Boots on the Ground, Wounded Warriors Canada, and Beyond the Blue. With these partnerships, we are removing barriers to services and normalizing access to mental healthcare as part of our everyday lives.

Support Through Transitions Officers under investigation by professional standards unit (PSB) reported feeling abandoned by the organization. The members felt cut off from resources that could help them in their recovery. Members under investigation by the special investigations unit (SIU)[5] said the process created unnecessary stress and left some feeling they have been found guilty before the process even began.

A very different type of stress is experienced by members transitioning from work to retirement. Some members struggle with a loss of identity. In addition, members who were experiencing psychological issues while working are likely to continue to struggle with these issues in retirement or have issues become prominent after years of avoidance and distraction. Members can also experience significant stress when transitioning from a specialist service to frontline uniform or into a new position and may require some additional supports through this process.

What We Are Doing The OPP provides specific training on signs and symptoms of operational stress injuries for members and for supervisors. Peer supporters and care navigators offer support to members and their families through transitions in and out of the workplace due to illness/injury. New recruits are provided with resiliency training, and psychological assessments and enhanced prehire and onboarding processes are in place for members in or transitioning to high-risk roles. Members in certain specialty units are part of a Health Check-in program wherein a job requirement is to meet with an internal or external regulated healthcare professional at least once per year. Attendance is mandatory while participation is voluntary; the primary purposes of the check-ins are relationship development with a clinician, decreased stigma, and increased self-awareness and psychoeducation.

[5] SIU is an independent civilian agency with a mandate to investigate police interactions resulting in serious injury, death, the discharge of a firearm at a person, or an allegation of sexual assault.

Supportive Policies and Processes Some policies and processes have the potential to inadvertently contribute to stigma surrounding mental health issues. Significant concerns were raised about the processes for removal and return of use of force. In addition, members who returned to work without their use of force reported finding themselves being assigned menial work and isolated from colleagues. Others found that despite being ready to return to work with workplace restrictions, they waited months, even years, to return. OPP members reported a lack of consultation and support mechanisms in place to guide the return-to-work process. Many felt abandoned and isolated, and far too often they ended up going back on leave. Many OPP members said that workplace conflicts were not resolved in a timely manner. The delays in arriving at a resolution contributed to members' stress and, in some cases, resulted in the members needing to take time off.

What We Are Doing Although continuous improvement in the area remains a high priority for us, the OPP has revised its Return to Work and Accommodations Policies and Processes and Removal and Return of Use of Force Policies and Processes. The hiring of an Occupational Doctor to handle Fit for Duty and Accommodations consultations has more clearly defined managers' roles with respect to following up with members on leave from the workplace.

The Healthy Workplace Team care navigators support members through workplace insurance and long-term disability insurance processes, while psychologists and mental health clinicians are available to provide consultation to supervisors and support to members throughout the return-to-work process. As of 2022, operational reintegration sergeants are also available for support through a graduated return to or stay-at-work process.

Mental Health Literacy OPP members struggling with their mental health reported experiencing varying levels of intolerance and resentment by colleagues and supervisors. Many also reported feeling isolated, ignored, and abandoned by their peers and the organization. Stigma was identified as a significant barrier to seeking help.

What We Are Doing The OPP provides ongoing mental health literacy training to all its members. In 2020–2021, all members were required to complete online suicide prevention skills training. Mental health training and education is being integrated into relevant Provincial Police Academy courses for new recruits, coach officers, and supervisors. Supervisors and managers are also receiving training on supporting their members and communication skills.

Continuous Improvement With an organization of almost 9600 members deployed across Ontario, it will take leadership, time, and support to ensure we get things right. Our commitment to continuous improvement will ensure that the ongoing evaluation of supports and programs is used to measure overall success. The OPP continues to expand and address the priorities surrounding mental health.

There have been many well-intentioned but incomplete interventions tried by many services, including my own, to support members. Increasing ready and timely access to culturally informed mental healthcare professionals and peer supporters is a necessary but not a sufficient step. We cannot focus solely on Band-aid supports "after the fact." To create a truly healthier workplace, day-to-day practices and interactions *must* take into account our members throughout every step. While exposure to trauma cannot be prevented for police service members, we can make changes in how leaders and members speak to each other, develop procedures that take into account member wellness needs (e.g., staffing levels), and ensure flexibility in policy implementation. While maintaining an unwavering commitment to public safety and our mission, with very few exceptions, administrative policy should rarely override consideration of our individual and collective members' need. This is not a "zero sum game": We as leaders can strive for operational excellence and hold members accountable for their actions while at the same time being mindful of individual factors and support our members.

What we do matters.

Together, we are making meaningful and effective changes to sustain a healthy and inclusive workplace. The ongoing dialog about mental health must continue. Our people are our greatest assets, and the mental health and physical safety of our OPP members are my top priority—and it is the only way we can effectively execute our mission and maintain public safety.

I close by issuing a personal call to action to anyone who is struggling with mental health—I hope you come forward to seek support and assistance; that is the greatest sign of strength and courage that any one of us can exhibit. We owe it to ourselves, and we owe it to each other to encourage others to come forward when help is needed. We will monitor our colleagues, friends, and family, and when we see signs and symptoms that they may be struggling, we will have those important open conversations. We are in this together—break the silence.

Acknowledgments

About the Ontario Provincial Police

The Ontario Provincial Police (OPP) is a division of the Ministry of the Solicitor General and is the police service of jurisdiction for Ontario. With a current membership of over 5,700 uniform members and 2,500 civilians, police services are provided to 328 of Ontario's 444 municipalities in areas spanning remote northern and First Nations communities to rural, farming, and urban centers. The OPP patrols more than one million square kilometers of land, waterways, and trails along with more than 131,000 kilometers of highways and roadways. The organization is responsible for the provision of a wide array of programs and services and the leadership of numerous multidisciplinary joint-force provincial initiatives to reduce harm and victimization. Over 14 million residents are served by the OPP.

Thomas Carrique, Commissioner, Ontario Provincial Police

Thomas Carrique became the 15th Commissioner of the Ontario Provincial Police on April 8, 2019.

Commissioner Carrique commenced his policing career with York Regional Police in 1990. He worked in a variety of roles including uniform patrol, criminal investigations, investigative services, traffic, marine, and public order. He progressed through the ranks and served as Deputy Chief of the Administration Branch, the Operations Branch, and the Investigations and Support Branch.

Commissioner Carrique holds a master's degree in leadership and training, with a specialty in justice and public safety, from Royal Roads University, and a certificate in terrorism studies from the University of St. Andrews in Scotland. He is a graduate of the National Policing Improvement Agency's International Commanders Program in the UK and the US Department of Justice Drug Unit Commanders Academy. He is currently a cochair of the Criminal Intelligence Service Canada National Executive Committee, and he is President of the Canadian Association of Chiefs of Police and serves on the board of directors for the Ontario Association of Chiefs of Police. In addition, he is an appointed member of the International Association of Chiefs of Police, Division of State and Provincial Police Executive Committee.

Commissioner Carrique is a recipient of the Police Exemplary Service Medal and the Queen Elizabeth II Diamond Jubilee Medal. He is also a Commander of the Order of Merit of the Police Forces as well as a Serving Brother of the Order of St. John Ambulance.

References

André Marin, Ombudsman of Ontario. In the Line of Duty. (2012, October). https://www.ombudsman.on.ca/Media/ombudsman/ombudsman/resources/Reports-on-Investigations/OPP-final-EN-accessible.pdf

Canadian Institute for Public Safety Research and Treatment (CIPSRT). (2019). *Glossary of terms: A shared understanding of the common terms used to describe psychological trauma* (version 2.1). Author. http://hdl.handle.net/10294/9055; https://www.cipsrt-icrtsp.ca/en/glossary/operational-stress-injury-osi

Carleton, R. N., Afifi, T. O., Turner, S., Taillieu, T., Duranceau, S., LeBouthillier, D. M., et al. (2017). Mental disorder symptoms among public safety personnel in Canada. *The Canadian Journal of Psychiatry, 63*(1), 54–64. https://doi.org/10.1177/0706743717723825. https://journals.sagepub.com/doi/pdf/10.1177/0706743717723825

Carleton, R. N., Afifi, T. O., Turner, S., Taillieu, T., LeBouthillier, D. M., Duranceau, S., et al. (2018). Suicidal ideation, plans, and attempts among public safety personnel in Canada. *Canadian Psychology/Psychologie Canadienne, 59*(3), 220–231. http://psycnet.apa.org/fulltext/2018-05339-001.pdf

Carleton, R. N., et al. (2020). Assessing the relative impact of diverse stressors among public safety personnel. *International Journal of Environmental Research and Public Health, 17*(4), Article 1234.

Elovainio, M., Kivimäki, M., Steen, N., & Kalliomäki-Levanto, T. (2000). Organizational and individual factors affecting mental health and job satisfaction: A multilevel analysis of job control and personality. *Journal of Occupational Health Psychology, 5*(2), 269.

Kalergis, K. I., & Molnar, B. E. (2017). *NCVRW creating a vicarious trauma-informed organization: Strategies for success* [Webinar]. Retrieved from https://ovc.ncjrs.gov/pdftxt/

Creating_a_Vicarious_Trauma-Informed_Organization_Strategies_for_Success_Recording_Presentation_508.pdf

Katsavouni, F., Bebetsos, E., Malliou, P., & Beneka, A. (2016). The relationship between burnout, PTSD symptoms and injuries in firefighters. *Occupational Medicine, 66*, 32–37. Retrieved from https://academic.oup.com/occmed/article/66/1/32/2750638

Mental Health Commission of Canada. (2018). *Research on suicide and its prevention: What the current evidence reveals and topics for future research.* Mental Health Commission of Canada. www.mentalhealthcommission.ca

Ontario Provincial Police Independent Review Panel: Final Report. (2019). Ontario Provincial Police Independent Review Panel: Final Report: Summary of recommendations | Ontario.ca

Queirós, C., et al. (2020). Job stress, burnout and coping in police officers: Relationships and psychometric properties of the Organizational Police Stress Questionnaire. *International Journal of Environmental Research and Public Health, 17*, Article 6718.

Regehr, C., & LeBlanc, V. (2017). PTSD, acute stress, performance and decision-making in emergency service workers. *Journal of the American Academy of Psychiatry and the Law, 45*, 184–192.

What Do You Know? Ensuring There Is Evidence to Support Meaningful Well-Being Interventions in UK Policing

Ian Hesketh

Introduction

In March 2021, the Police in England and Wales employed 220,519 people (UK Gov, 2022). This is made up of 135,301 police officers, 75,934 police staff and designated officers, 9284 police community support officers, and 9174 special constables and 8014 police support volunteers. We use 31st March 2021 as the datum due to the fact the police uplift programme, with a target of an extra 20,000 officers and staff, renders it difficult to apply any accurate number until complete. So, it is at least this number. A further caveat is this is the 43 Home Office forces of England and Wales and there are a further 2 territorial forces, Police Scotland (17,289 police officers) and the Police Service of Northern Ireland (PSNI with a further 6962 police officers), as well as 3 specialist police forces in the United Kingdom.

Measuring Well-Being

The National Police Wellbeing Service is discussed in its' entirety in a further chapter of this book. What we discuss here is how we go about measuring how our population think and feel about their lives in policing. This is done through the lens of a national survey of all police and police staff. The first UK National Police Wellbeing Survey was designed to assess the current state of well-being (US—*Wellness*) from the perspective of the policing workforce itself. It was conducted within the 43 Home Office forces in England and Wales. These account for the entirety of UK Home Office forces, although there are several other "non-Home Office" forces

I. Hesketh (✉)
Alliance Manchester Business School, The University of Manchester, Manchester, UK
e-mail: ian.hesketh-2@manchester.ac.uk

K. Papazoglou, K. Kamkar (eds.), *Multi-faceted Approaches to Challenges and Coping in Law Enforcement*, https://doi.org/10.1007/978-3-031-62825-2_4

(EG Police Scotland, Police Service of Northern Ireland, and British Transport Police). The research was conducted by independent researchers from Durham University Business School, led by Professor Les Graham.

Purpose

The purpose of this research was to establish the current state of well-being via the voice of those employed within UK policing, including both police officers and police staff. The aims of the first survey of its kind in the UK were to establish key measures for workplace factors, staff attitudes, motivation, and well-being. These can be tracked over time and can provide findings that can be used to inform, design, and deliver future well-being programs. These programs include leadership, resilience, and how to create an environment in which those involved in policing can pursue careers that are high in meaning and are purposeful, the tenets of well-being (Hesketh & Cooper, 2017a, b). The survey was designed in order that every member of the police service can contribute in a safe environment with the knowledge that the findings will be used to inform future practice.

This chapter will outline the content of designing, developing, delivering, analyzing, and communicating the survey findings. Further, the initial design and piloting of well-being interventions focus on evidence-based meaningful approaches that directly address the findings from the surveys. An initial evaluation overview will be included and a vision of what the future may look like, including lessons learned, to inform the surveys that followed. At the time of writing, we are undertaking the fourth wave of surveys.

It should be noted that the first survey was conducted, in its entirety, before the COVID-19 outbreak and consisted of 34,500 useable responses. The second survey was conducted during COVID-19 (n = 22 k) and the third as we emerged from the pandemic (n = 37 k). The fourth is being conducted as we are returning to normality and all the fiscal challenges being faced within that return.

So, What Is the Evidence Base?

In all spheres of policing, gathering the evidence to support a claim is critical. Measuring the workforce, our people fleet (Hesketh & Cooper, 2017a, b), is no different. The national survey is designed to assess the current state of well-being from the perspective of the whole policing workforce. Briner et al. (2009) suggest there are four sources of evidence that inform, in their case, management practice. The aim of the surveys is to provide this evidence for a host of stakeholders, including the workforce themselves. The factors Briner et al. list are as follows:

1. Practitioner expertise

2. Organizational data
3. Research findings
4. Stakeholder voice

We suggest that the survey garners all four of these factors to inform management practice and stakeholder query. We then take these findings to test and evaluate interventions that address the issues raised within the survey. We will discuss these in more detail later in this chapter.

We proposed that in these times of burgeoning Internet media channels, the use of all forms of social media can also contribute, or at least heavily influence, decision-making based on professional judgement in management practice—it could be argued this is stakeholder voice, though not all commentators are strictly stakeholders of course. We suggest that professional practice is about recognizing these individuals' expertise or opinion, listening to it and identifying what meaning and in what context it can be applied to. Supporting our previous studies, we suggest that this then does not leave the most important asset, that being the staff, feeling like a unit of production (Hesketh & Williams, 2017) that is constantly tampered with. That is, they have no say and decisions are made at the whim of the public rhetoric or executive teams flip-flopping. Here, we suggest, lies the crux of surveying and, as you will hear, can also be measured, of course!

What We Measured and What It Told Us

In this part of the chapter, we will outline what is measured, the purpose of the measurement, and how it relates to our overall aim to improve the well-being of all those involved in policing. The elements are ordered alphabetically, so no inference should be drawn in terms of priority. Arguably, each element is critical, and hence why we include them. It should be noted that not all elements have been measured in all waves of surveying. However, we have settled on a standardized set, for now. It is almost certain that these will change as new challenges emerge and new validated scales become more suitable to measure law enforcement realms. It should be acknowledged that the survey is meticulously prepared, with a great deal of planning around what is included. The work of Professor Les Graham, the principal investigator, at Durham University Business School in the United Kingdom has been critical to ensuring the survey is valid and reliable. It must be acknowledged that the success of the survey is largely down to the huge effort of Professor Graham and his team. In particular, Natalie Brown and Marisa Plater have worked tirelessly with Professor Graham to structure, test, and format the below into validated question sets. This unquestionably makes this survey a robust instrument that police forces can trust to provide the evidence base to much of their people strategies. We have seen that firsthand. The below descriptions are taken directly from the three rounds of surveys we have conducted thus far. At the time of going to press, we are undertaking the fourth wave of surveys, again being conducted by the excellent team at Durham University Business School. The full details of all the surveys are available publicly and can be found in the links referenced at the end of this chapter.

What Good Looks Like

Anxiety and depression symptoms are on the more serious end and very often lead to serious illness and long-term abstractions from the workplace. Therefore, high scoring returns in these aspects should be addressed very seriously. Anxiety refers to feelings of tension and nervousness, worried thoughts, and physical changes in relation to thinking about an uncertain outcomes or impending events. Anxiety is very common but also can be very damaging and difficult to recover from. Often the role of a line manager can cause this, not managing workloads, inappropriate tasking, and so on. Conversely, a caring line manager can help greatly with anxiety, especially kind and sympathetic managers with good social skills and the ability to spot the signs something is amiss with an employee. Depression refers to feelings of sadness, despair, discouragement, and worthlessness. Symptoms of anxiety and depression tend to be highly linked. Lower scores on these measures are much more desirable and are indicative of a good workplace, good comradery, and good line management. Good workplaces shine in respect to these measures. In our 2021–2022 survey overall, reported levels remain moderately high for symptoms of anxiety and moderate for symptoms of depression with no significant difference in average scores between police officers and police staff (Graham et al., 2022).

Sleep

Disturbed Sleep and Insufficient Sleep. You would like to think that the importance of sleep for restorative daily functioning is common sense and that police prioritize this in their working lives. However, the reality is far from this picture. Survey after survey records poor sleep quantity and quality as off the scale in terms of how poor it is. It has remained a top priority from almost the beginning to going to press, with very slight improvements beginning to show as a result of many, many initiatives, programs of education, and monitoring activities. It is well documented that exposure to emotionally stressful situations has been shown to be related to reduced sleep quality and higher levels of sleep disturbance. Unfortunately, the nature of policing does not afford officers and staff freedom from repeated exposure to these highly charged and emotionally draining situations. In fact, it is quite the opposite. To that extent, when reduced sleep quality occurs, sensitivity to emotional and other stressful situations increases, which can exacerbate the impact of stressors on individual emotional energy and well-being. We have previously described policing as being high in terms of emotional labor. A huge concern for the service, particularly associated with shift work, is the lack of recovery time available which can have serious impacts on individuals' health, well-being, and performance. Our measure is to ask respondents how often they had less than 6 h of sleep and how frequently they had experienced sleep disturbance. This is explored through the form of restlessness, difficulty falling asleep, or unintentional early waking. Lower reported frequencies of disturbed sleep and insufficient sleep are more desirable, but definitely not the general response. In fact, in our first UK police national survey (n = 35 k), 45% of police officers reported having less than 6 h sleep per night. The following year, with interventions, this had reduced to a still very high 40% of police officers (Graham et al., 2022). We are working on further sleep related interventions to improve this picture with several strands we will detail later in this chapter.

Energy

Emotional energy is vital to individuals' well-being, particularly in the life and challenges in an occupation like policing. Emotional energy can be considered as the amount of emotional and mental energy individuals have available to them to meet the daily demands and challenges they face in their roles. Especially when we consider the mental and physical challenges of policing, this is critical, as low levels of emotional energy are manifested by both physical fatigue and a sense of feeling psychologically and emotionally "drained" at work. There is a plethora of prior research that has found that low emotional energy levels are related to reduced organizational commitment. Again, in an occupation such as policing, this is undesirable. Other direct consequences have been described as lower productivity and performance, reduced engagement, ill-health, decreased physical and mental well-being, increased absenteeism and turnover intentions, and lower levels of persistence in the face of difficulties. These are all problematic in any organization and especially significant in policing. The measurement of this has allowed us to understand in greater detail how officers and staff are feeling about their working life and the impact it is having on them. Turnover rates, recruitment, and ill-health retirements are a major concern for most police departments, not least because of the impact and sheer costs involved. For example, following the previous slight increase reported in the 2020/2021 results, police officer emotional energy in the United Kingdom has declined in the past 12 months and is now at a similar average level to that found in the 2019/2020 survey (Graham et al., 2022).

Incivility

Experienced workplace incivility can be thought of as a generalized form of low-intensity, subtle, harmful behavior directed toward others, which can be verbal (being rude or disrespectful) or nonverbal (excluding or ignoring someone).

Individuals in our survey are asked how frequently they had experienced being treated in a condescending manner by someone in their force while at work over the past 12 months. Lower reported frequencies are more desirable. In 2019, 67% of police officers reported having experienced workplace incivility. This reduced during the pandemic, perhaps obviously, to 62% but increased to 75% following the pandemic years. Another area of concern was that it was far more prevalent in the lower ranks, less so at higher ranks. In terms of police staff (civilian roles), the patterns were similar but not as high, with pre pandemic levels of 61%, pandemic years at 52%, and post pandemic reported at 64%. Of course, experiencing incivility in the workplace leads to lower well-being, so it is serious in nature and undesirable in any workplace (Graham et al., 2022).

Fatigue

Fatigue is an overwhelming sense of being tired, lacking energy, and feeling exhausted. Fatigue arises through engaging in demanding activities, of which there are many in policing—both physical and psychological. While fatigue is related to emotional exhaustion, it differs in that it can be relieved by using compensation mechanisms such as working more slowly or taking adequate rest and gaining sufficient sleep. Our strong investment in sector specific sleep research is a testimony to this. Further, prior research has shown that fatigue is associated with reduced communication skills, reduced ability to handle stress, increased risk-taking, reduced decision-making ability, increased errors of judgment and likelihood to have an accident, an inability to recall details, a lack of attention and vigilance, reduced performance, and increased absence from work. A lower score on this measure is more desirable, and high scores are indicative of a poorly run working environment. Our survey findings for 2021/2022 found that levels of general fatigue were found to be higher for police officers than staff, with 29.6% of officers indicating very high levels of fatigue. 21.9% of police staff indicated the same very high levels of fatigue (Graham et al., 2022).

The Great Resignation

Intention to Quit. We asked individuals whether they were thinking about, or looking for, alternative employment and whether they intend to quit the police force in the near future. While prior research has shown that intention to quit is moderately associated with individuals leaving, it can be considered as a way of assessing their levels of disengagement and withdrawal from their job. We often characterize this as an intention to be awkward or to withdraw discretionary effort. The consequences of this measure can be an effective work to rule. This leads to an uneasiness in the workforce and can make the working environment intolerable. Therefore, a lower score on this measure is more desirable. In our second year, survey intention to quit lowered in both police officers and police staff. We considered this to be as a consequence of the pandemic, where those working in policing felt their jobs were worthwhile and contributing strongly to society. In well-being terms, they felt higher levels of meaning and purpose in their work. We also noted that workload levels had considerably lowered across the piste, with less calls for service. Of course, everyone was asked to stay at home so this was to be expected. However, as the restrictions have lifted and we are returning back to normal levels of calls for service and workloads have increased significantly, we have seen a sharp rise in the third round of surveys in this measure. We also note that intention to quit is at its lowest levels in individuals with less than a year's service and increases gradually as tenure rises (Graham et al., 2022). Again, this may seem a natural development; however, we must find ways to address this, and a lot is down to good supervision, personal resilience, and a suitable working environment.

Satisfaction

Job satisfaction is defined as how content an individual is with their job. We measured a single dimension of affective job satisfaction to represent an overall emotional feeling that individuals have about their job. In the surveys, we have seen a steady decline in job satisfaction among both police staff and police officers in the United Kingdom (Graham et al., 2022). We also know that hindrance stressors have a detrimental impact on job satisfaction and therefore gives us a course of action to improve this area of work. One of our main streams of work for 2022–2023 will be the removal or reduction of hindrance stressors as the main thrust of work, developing a service improvement and stress reduction program (SISR).

Life satisfaction is an individual's judgement of their life and is dependent on their assessment and views of their personal circumstances. It is often a gauge of subjective well-being, or Hedonic well-being, that of pleasure or happiness. This judgment takes place against an internal standard which they have set for themselves. It can be considered as a measure of an individual's subjective well-being and a comment on their feeling of overall satisfaction with life. The survey findings supported the view that when police officers and staff felt their work was having a positive impact, their life satisfaction scores were higher. As previously discussed, this was particularly relevant during the period of lockdown. Other areas that impact on life satisfaction are feelings that individuals are being treated fairly and receiving organizational support. Conversely, when people experience incivility, this is negatively associated with life satisfaction. In our last survey, police officers reported moderately high life satisfaction, continuing an upward trend from our first survey, and police staff reported high levels of life satisfaction, again continuing an upward trend from the first survey (Graham et al., 2022).

Feeling Supported

Perceived organizational support (POS) refers to individuals' beliefs regarding the degree to which they feel the organization values their contributions and cares about their well-being. It also refers to a feeling of assurance that the organization will provide support when individuals face particularly difficult or challenging circumstances when carrying out their duties. This is particularly important in terms of attraction and recruitment into the service. We have found recruits are willing to talk about their own feelings and emotions far more than their predecessors. However, they do have the expectation that if they ask for help, it is available. When individuals feel valued, their socioemotional needs of respect, being cared for, and receiving approval will be met, and they will reciprocate with higher levels of discretionary effort and felt obligation. The importance of discretionary effort in policing is discussed in a further paper (see Hesketh et al., 2017). POS is more strongly related to social exchange rather than economic exchange because it is most affected by discretionary actions by the organization rather than as a result of external constraints, such as government regulations. Perceptions of positive support from the organization affect an individual's relationship with the organization and have an important impact on individuals' well-being and commitment toward the organization. Worryingly, the latest survey reported police officers having moderately low scores in POS, with police staff having only moderate. However, volunteers reported high average levels (Graham et al., 2022).

Physical Well-Being

Physical well-being refers to the overall condition and functioning of the body. Physical well-being has been linked to disease management, nutrition, and physical exercise. Respondents rated their general physical health over a 3-month period. For both police officers and staff, the first survey reported the highest levels of physical well-being, with a drop in the pandemic year and slight recovery in the third wave study. Shift workers reported poorer physical health also (Graham et al., 2020, 2021, 2022). We have a number of initiatives running looking at various aspects of physical health, including trialing of "Whoop" bands, actigraphy (see James et al., 2021), and Move More challenges (see Oliver et al., 2021).

Contributing

Process improvement behavior is a set of proactive actions aimed at implementing positive, constructive change through finding solutions to organizational problems, making small changes to working procedures and the introduction of new working methods. It is based on personal initiative and conscious decision-making, rather than a formal requirement, and is therefore thought of as an extra-role behavior (discretionary effort—discussed above). Generally, these were reported as high, with higher ranks (police officers) and grade (police staff) reporting higher levels the higher the rank or grade. Volunteers, special constables, and police community support officers also rated high on this measure (Graham et al., 2022).

Motivation

Prosocial Motivation. Individuals with strong prosocial values are motivated by a core desire to help and benefit others, which influences their actions and decisions. It can be viewed as the antipode to the better known antisocial behavior used to describe disruptive behaviors in communities in the United Kingdom and on which a lot of recent legislation has relied upon to address persistent nuisance incidents. For this measure, we asked whether individuals feel motivated to have a positive impact by helping and benefiting others in society through their work. We didn't measure this area in our first survey, but the second and third waves of study saw a slight decrease (although still high) in this in police officers and police staff (Graham et al., 2022). We posited this may be due to the increase in workloads as we came out of lockdown in the United Kingdom as it is associated with fatigue and intentions to quit. This is another measure which increases with grade or rank.

Resting

Psychological detachment from work refers to an individual's state of mind when they are not working and their ability to distance themselves from job-related issues, problems, or opportunities. This is closely related to phenomena such as presenteeism (Johns, 2010) and leaveism (Hesketh & Cooper, 2014). It demonstrates an individual's ability to switch off and distance themselves from their job, not only physically but also mentally. A very positive finding is that average scores for psychological detachment for both officers and staff have improved since the 2020/2021 survey (Graham et al., 2022). There is strong research evidence for the importance of psychological detachment in the recovery from work stress. Such recovery experiences help employees replenish cognitive resources lost due to work demands, which further increases their psychological health and life satisfaction and decreases the negative impacts from stressors on employees' well-being and performance.

Psychological Need Satisfaction. Research has suggested that people have three universal psychological needs of autonomy, competence, and relatedness, which need to be satisfied to maintain optimal performance and well-being. We use the pneumonic CAR in our leadership programs to illustrate this, utilizing the survey findings to provide working examples of self-determination theory (Deci & Ryan,

2000). Autonomy relates to feeling able to act and make choices that reflect one's personal beliefs and values. Competence relates to an individual's feelings of being skillful, effective, and able to make a contribution. Relatedness refers to a need to feel a sense of belonging and being part of a team where they feel respected and valued. Psychological needs can be thought of as nutrients that are essential for individual's adjustment, integrity, and growth. Satisfaction of psychological needs are essential for individual well-being. When the fulfilment of psychological needs is frustrated, this results in individuals becoming defensive or passive and suffering from ill-health. We asked individuals the extent to which each of the psychological needs are met, in general, while at work over the past 3 months.

Being Valued

Sense of Being Valued. Value is defined as the relative importance or worth that people feel they deserve. We asked individuals to rate the extent to which they feel valued by their coworkers, supervisor, force, and the public. The survey results from these areas are fascinating. For police officers and staff, coworker and supervisor sense of being valued was high. However, the sense of being valued by their own force and by members of the public was low. Further, all of these are stable over all 3 years of surveying, with the exception of the public. This has seen a steady decline over the years for police officers, but for police staff, it has increased. There is also an enormous gulf between feeling valued by the public in terms of ranks, with higher ranks reporting feeling far more valued than their lower ranked colleagues. This was not the case with police staff (Graham et al., 2020, 2021, 2022).

Leadership

Supervisor listen signals to individuals that their supervisor is open, interested, and supportive, leading to employees feeling more comfortable when approaching and talking to their supervisor. The surveys, reassuringly, reported these as high across the board (Graham et al., 2022).

Supportive leadership is very much our approach of choice as we see real impact in the tenets of this approach, mainly that it is strongly associated with well-being. Supportive leadership stresses the importance of personal integrity and serving others, such as employees and communities. It focuses on the development of people to their fullest potential through an understanding of each person's different characteristics, strengths, and interests. We include supportive leadership as the core of the majority of our training inputs. Supportive leaders serve as role models, build trust, and provide feedback and resources to their people. It is argued that supportive leadership combats negative outcomes associated with the promotion of self-interest which underlies many incidents of unethical behavior. Supportive leadership behavior includes showing compassion for their team members and protecting them from harm in the workplace through the reduction of exposure to hindrance stressors (discussed above), incivility, and ostracism. Our supportive leadership measure is new, and in our last survey, we were pleased to see that both police officers and police staff reported high levels on this measure (Graham et al., 2022).

Belonging

Team belonging can be considered as whether individuals feel accepted by other members of their work team and whether they have a sense of belonging to their team and feel connected to team members. In our latest survey, this measure was reported as high in both police officers and police staff, regardless of tenure, rank, or grade (Graham et al., 2022).

Vision Clarity. Individuals were asked their opinions on how clear the organization's vision is to them, whether it has defined objectives, and whether it is easy to understand. Interestingly, the survey reported this notably increasing with rank and grade in both police officers and police staff. However, we have measured this only on the one occasion, so the fourth wave study will make for a more insightful diagnosis.

Engagement

Work Engagement. We have previous experience in researching engagement, especially around the relationship with discretionary effort—see, for example, Hesketh et al. (2017). Engagement is a measure of an individual's personal expression of their self-in-role. A person is engaged in their work when they are able to express their authentic self and are willing to invest their emotional, cognitive, and physical energies into their work and job roles. To do this requires them to feel that the work has meaning, a key tenet of well-being, that they feel safe, and that they have the necessary resources. Improved engagement can lead to higher individual performance, enhanced well-being, and reduced staff turnover. Reducing turnover has recently come to be one of the top objectives for most police forces in the United Kingdom—especially around police recruits. The changes to terms and conditions have had a detrimental impact on both recruitment and tenure. Although reported as high in police officers and police staff alike, work engagement gradually decreases with tenure. We have measured this twice and both tell a similar story (Graham et al., 2021, 2022).

Key Survey Findings

As part of our commitment to engaging with the whole police service, we produce a series of roadshows and presentations outlining the key findings for the surveys. These are very often introduced in the form of info graphs. We also detail what evidence-based interventions we have ongoing or which we hope to fund in the future. If there are no existing evidence-based interventions, we collaborate with academics, businesses, and practitioners to establish what may be useful to test. The key findings from our latest survey are outlined below and thus keep or interest in sleep and fatigue very high on our agenda:

- Emotional energy for police officers increased at the start of the pandemic (2019 → 2020 survey) with a small-medium effect size, but this has dropped back in the 2021 survey with a medium effect size and is now at just slightly below the average level reported in 2019. There were no major changes across the 3 years for police staff.
- Fatigue was newly introduced as a measure in the 2020 survey. A slight increase in fatigue is evident for police officers with a small effect size. There was no significant change for police staff.
- Only very small changes in scores were found for sleep quality, but this suggests a slight decline (i.e., increased frequencies of sleep disturbance and having less than 6 h of sleep per night) in scores for police officers between the 2020 and 2021 national surveys (not significant for police staff).

Interventions and Evaluations

One of the interventions introduced was a multifaceted approach to what was by far our most worrying of findings, that of sleep and fatigue. The results from our first ever national police well-being survey in 2019 told us very clearly that fatigue is a big issue within policing. It identified that 45% of police officers and 30% of police staff reported sleeping less than 6 h per night very often or all of the time and that people working shifts experience poor sleep quality more frequently with 27% of police officers and 25% of police staff reporting disturbed sleep. In terms of sleep measures, this was in both quantity and quality. After our first survey, we immediately onboarded a Chief Inspector Police Officer to take the lead on this stream of work. Having just completed her PhD, Yvonne Taylor was perfectly placed as both a senior police officer with considerable service on the front line and a recent academic with a great understanding of the contemporary landscape of sleep research. With support from the rest of the team, she immediately got to work building an evidence base of what works for the police in terms of improving sleep. As above, you can see the worrying levels of sub 6-h sleep across the board. This is the cutoff where we know regular exposure leads to numerous physical and mental health challenges. We worked closely with Professor Steven Lockley of Surrey (UK) and Harvard University (USA), testing and developing the sleep alertness and fatigue in emergency responders (SAFER) program. You can see an outline of the program at SAFER program YouTube. We also looked at sleep habits more closely in collaboration with Washington State University. They embarked on a study using actigraphy, wearable technology that accurately records sleep quality and quantity (James et al., 2021). On top of this, we commissioned a number of sleep webinars and online events with a UK expert, Dr. Sophie Bostock (see Oscar Kilo—Better Sleep program). All of these programs have undergone independent evaluation to ensure validity. Following this, they are moved into the final element of our service provision. It should be noted that we are also seeking to explore economic evaluation of some of our psychological programs also—see, for example, McCrone et al. (2018).

Business as Usual

The diagram below clearly illustrates how we take information from our survey to inform and develop interventions. These interventions are then robustly tested and evaluated. If they are proven to be successful or show signs of promising practice, we develop further iterations. Incrementally they are then scaled up and if proven introduced as business as usual. We take care to monitor in the early years to ensure they both continue to be effective and relevant (Fig. 1).

Fig. 1 The NPWS capability model. (Hesketh, 2023)

By way of example, future surveys will measure the impact of our superb OK9 well-being dogs and the impact they are having on officers and staff. Supporting the above proposition, social media commentary is extremely positive. What we need to establish is the relationship with factors mentioned in our measurements above. We do this by using study methodology similar to that we used to look at workplace stressors and the impact on exhaustion and engagement and the role of hindrance stressors (Lockey et al., 2021). This helps us to focus on the important well-being impact the dogs have—we are making assumptions up to now without evidence of such.

Other exciting workplace initiatives that have arisen out of our evidence-based research, using survey data have included our efforts on the Physical wellbeing front, see for example Oliver et al. (2021). Our research on psychological risk management, see for example Tehrani and Hesketh (2018). The use of mental health apps, see for example Marston et al. (2020). All these add weight to the use of robust evidence-based approaches based on data from end users of the interventions.

Conclusions

The above diagram and accompanying dialog clearly illustrate the cycle of bringing research into practice. Using academic rigor and employee voice, we have managed to present how an evidence-based approach to modeling the thoughts, feelings, and experience of serving police officers and staff in the United Kingdom can help make meaningful changes to the working environment. These changes make things better for those who work in policing. In addition to the obvious links to the service, those officers and staff provide a better service to the public. We can illustrate this also! The link to personal resilience and effective leadership is also clearly defined, as without either, these approaches will not prove as effective.

The National Wellbeing Survey was designed to assess the current state of well-being from the perspective of the policing workforce within the 43 Home Office forces in England and Wales. The purpose of this research is to provide an evidence base to support interventions introduced by the National Police Wellbeing Service. Responses were collected over three annual surveys, with a fourth ongoing as we go to press.

A final word must go to the excellent friendships, collaborations, knowledge sharing, and hard work of the other contributors in this book. I consider all of them to be friends and over many years have enjoyed enormously our interactions at conferences, online and in bars, restaurants, and coffee bars around the world. This global network provides exciting debate and imbues a provocation to get this right on behalf of British policing. Long may these relationships continue, I cannot thank you enough.

References

Briner, R. B., Denyer, D., & Rousseau, D. M. (2009). Evidence- based management: Concept cleanup time? *Academy of Management Perspectives, 23*(4), 19–32.
Deci, E. L., & Ryan, R. M. (2000). The "what" and "why" of goal pursuits: Human needs and the self-determination of behavior. *Psychological Inquiry, 11*(4), 227–268.
Graham, L., Brown, N., Plater, M., Gracey, S., Legate, N., & Weinstein, N. (2020, March). *National Policing Wellbeing Survey 2019: Summary of evidence and insights*. Durham University. Available on the National Police Wellbeing Service website: https://oscarkilo.org.uk/fatigue-to-be-tackled-following-first-ever-national-police-wellbeing-survey/
Graham, L., Plater, M., Brown, N., & Gracey, S. (2021, March). *National Policing Wellbeing Survey 2020: Summary of evidence and insights*. Durham University. Available on the National Police Wellbeing Service website: https://oscarkilo.org.uk/national-wellbeing-survey-results-published/
Graham, L., Plater, M., & Brown, N. (2022). *National Police Wellbeing Survey 2021/22*. Accessed: https://www.oscarkilo.org.uk/news/national-police-wellbeing-survey-2021
Hesketh, I. (2023). *The National Police Wellbeing Service (NPWS) Capability Model*. Created to illustrate the working process employed for research for NPWS. Unpublished.
Hesketh, I., & Cooper, C. (2014). Leaveism at work. *Occupational Medicine, 64*(3), 146–147.
Hesketh, I., & Cooper, C. (2017a). *Managing health and well-being in the public sector: A guide to best practice*. Routledge Psychology Press.
Hesketh, I., & Cooper, C. (2017b). Measuring the people fleet: General analysis, interventions and needs. *Strategic HR Review, 16*(1), 17–23. Emerald.
Hesketh, I., & Williams, E. (2017). A new canteen culture: Social media as evidence in Policing. *Policing, 11*, 346.
Hesketh, I., Cooper, C., & Ivy, J. (2017). Well-being and engagement: The key to unlocking discretionary effort? *Policing, 11*(1), 62–73. Oxford University Press.
James, L., James, S., & Hesketh, I. (2021). Evaluating the effectiveness of the fatigue and shift working risk management strategy for UK Home Office police forces: A pilot study. *International Journal of Emergency Services*. Emerald.
Johns, G. (2010). Presenteeism in the workplace: A review and research agenda. *Journal of Organizational Behavior, 31*(4), 519–542.
Lockey, S., Graham, L., Zheng, X., Hesketh, I., Plater, M., & Gracey, S. (2021). The impact of workplace stressors on exhaustion and work engagement in Policing. *Police Journal: Theory, Practice and Principles, 95*(1), 190. Sage.
Marston, H., Hadley, R., Pike, G., & Hesketh, I. (2020). Games for health & mental health apps for police & blue light personnel: A scoping review. *Games for Health Journal: Research, Development and Clinical Applications. Police Journal: Theory, Practice and Principles*. Sage.
McCrone, P., Rost, F., Koeser, L., et al. (2018). The economic cost of treatment resistant depression to patients referred to specialist services. *Journal of Mental Health, 27*(6), 567–573.
Oliver, H., Owen, O., Copeland, R., Hesketh, I., Jukes, M., Chadd, K., & Rocca, M. (2021). Proof of concept and feasibility of the app-based #SWPMoveMore challenge: Impacts on physical activity and wellbeing in a police population. *Police Journal: Theory, Practice and Principles, 95*(1), 170. Sage.
Tehrani, N., & Hesketh, I. (2018). The role of psychological screening for emergency service responders. *International Journal of Emergency Services*. Emerald, *8*, 4. https://doi.org/10.1108/IJES-04-2018-0021
UK Gov. (2022). *National Statistics—Police Workforce England and Wales: 31 March 2021 Second Edition*. Available at: https://www.gov.uk/government/statistics/police-workforce-england-and-wales-31-march-2021/police-workforce-england-and-wales-31-march-2021. Accessed 13 Aug 2022.

The Intersections of Trauma in Police Officers and Offenders

Dale McFee, Glen Klose, and Lauren Wozny

Do not ask what is wrong with them; ask what happened to them. This common saying in the public safety personnel community is often stated when a police officer, paramedic, firefighter, or correctional officer is thought to be difficult, angry, or quick to upset. It softens any judgment around why someone acts the way they do after working in a trauma-exposed workplace. Within this statement lies acknowledgment that if we recognize a person's history and prior trauma, we can understand the causes of their negative behavior and how to best support them. The same can be said of the members of the public that police officers interact with, including offenders. This is not to excuse or justify the behaviors of either but to better understand and humanize each other.

When considering how trauma affects the brain, the behavioral outcomes, and how it influences a person's reality, these two groups may have more in common than either would care to admit. Support that truly recognizes individual exposure to trauma is the most effective way to reintegrate individuals into the groups they seek to remain a part of. Trauma-informed activities such as yoga or the inclusion of safe space locations or groups for trauma-affected or marginalized individuals are some examples of that recognition. In a law-enforcement context, this includes trauma-informed policing and a more compassionate approach by police officers. Acknowledgment and support of an offender's prior trauma may aid in that person's effective reintegration into society after a period of criminality or incarceration. In the case of officers, it may mean the effective return to a specific team or set of duties.

This chapter does not seek to oversimplify the individual experiences of either police officers or offenders, nor to make broad comparisons of the two vastly different groups. Rather, it seeks to bring to light the areas in which both may be inclined to empathize with the circumstances that challenge the other in their pursuit of

D. McFee (✉) · G. Klose · L. Wozny
Edmonton Police Service, Edmonton, AB, Canada
e-mail: dale.mcfee@edmontonpolice.ca

K. Papazoglou, K. Kamkar (eds.), *Multi-faceted Approaches to Challenges and Coping in Law Enforcement*, https://doi.org/10.1007/978-3-031-62825-2_5

overcoming the barriers that individual trauma can present. This chapter will explore common intersections with a focus on the deterioration of cognitive function (decision-making) when a person has post-traumatic stress disorder (PTSD) and the biological effects of stress on the brain and body.

Adherence to Social Norms

To understand the intersections of trauma in these two groups, we should first understand how social norms and factors inhibiting adherence to them can impact an individual. In society there are generalized social norms based on personally intrinsic values or external community expectations, some of which are based in informal understanding and others which are formalized into rules and laws (Baier, 2013). Depending on the nature, individual transgressions against these norms can be met with sanctions such as disapproval and alienation or criminal charges and fines.

In recent years, social media platforms have become a prolific behavioral control mechanism by way of widespread condemnation for those perceived or found to be in contravention of society's written and unwritten expectations. Online platforms have given rise to the use of techniques like shaming, trolling, and doxxing to regulate perceived immoralities (Reeves & Ingraham, 2019). This is especially prevalent when the post content, photo, or video creates an emotional reaction in those viewing it (Guadagno et al., 2013). Social media content involving crime, victimization, or perceived transgressions by law enforcement often receives widespread attention from both social and traditional media platforms due to the response it elicits from those viewing it—specifically in how the actions viewed align with or are in contravention of their individual moral codes.

Smaller social groups within broader society have their own moral codes that passively or actively control the actions of those within the group. Members of these smaller groups may align with each other due to factors that inform their identity such as nationality, geography, race, gender, religion, profession, or even criminality. The establishment of such in-groups, and contrasting out-groups, is central to social identity theory and how one constructs their sense of self (Tajfel & Turner, 1979). Each group has expectations of their members surrounding aspects like behavior, communication, respect, work ethic, and how they interact with those of other (opposing) groups. While the penalty for stepping outside the norms of a smaller group may not be as formal as criminal charges, the means for groups to control those within them can have severe and long-lasting impacts. Criminal groups may use violence or threats of violence to control members, while other groups may rely on ostracization or other alienation techniques.

While most within a group will abide by the expectations set upon them, there are those that either choose not to conform or do not have the ability to do so based on prior experiences or trauma. Transgressions by in-group members often will be judged harshly which can further alienate those already struggling (Bettache et al.,

2019). While some may be quick to vilify those that do not have the ability to conform to group expectations, it is important that society explore the individual factors for these outliers to properly support them. This can be said for both those that defy the law or individual police officers that step outside the boundaries of behavioral expectations.

How Trauma Surfaces in Offenders

It is well established that those engaging in criminal activity often have a history of trauma, adverse childhood experiences, mental health issues, or addiction (Wolff & Shi, 2012). There is a growing expectation that before sentencing, a convicted individual's history and prior trauma be recognized by the courts. An example of this is a document called a Gladue report where, under section 718.2 (e) of Canada's Criminal Code, an indigenous offender's personal history of discrimination, abuse, and poverty and the effects of the residential school system are taken into consideration. Those that have trauma in their lives can be challenged with relationships, self-regulation, decision-making, and communication, which are often factors informing their actions (Wolff & Shi, 2012).

For example, children who suffer in chaotic housing situations or witness abuse in the home may struggle with genuine human connection and relationships later in life. These individuals may not feel safe in adulthood due to their long-standing history of instability and being unable to find safety with those who should have cared for them during their formative years. Without a model for healthy relationships, these children may grow into adults without the ability to trust others and build healthy social circles or interpersonal connections. Unstable environments hamper their ability to learn social cues, which help decipher others' intentions and aid in communication (McLaughlin & Lambert, 2017; Shepherd & Wild, 2014). For those in such circumstances, a good-natured joke may be misinterpreted as an insult, or an innocuous comment may be seen as a challenge to confrontation. The inability for an adult to decipher another person's intentions due to a lack of safety as a child can be attributed to environmental factors creating a substantial gap in their growth and development.

Those that struggle to recognize social cues can quickly become ostracized. This exacerbates an individual's situation further as they have increasingly less opportunity to integrate into society and practice the skills that would gain them admittance into the groups they wish to be part of. This divergence can turn into anger and resentment, which may manifest into acts of violence or verbal outbursts (Ren et al., 2018). Those that find themselves on the fringes of society run the risk of a dangerous thinking trap: "I did a bad thing, so I am a bad person." They may internalize the belief that they are not part of the greater group because they are a bad person as opposed to a person that was never properly supported and taught social skills. When they lose their temper in a social predicament because of an inability to read a situation or regulate their body from years of prior trauma or an unsafe environment, the belief that they are unworthy is pervasive.

When society vilifies or judges those that engage in criminal behavior or neglect to comply with social expectations, it fails to recognize that the root of a person's behavior likely developed years or decades prior (Roy, 2001). Those that did grow up in healthy situations may struggle to understand how segments of society could go against social norms and engage in criminal behavior, victimize others, or suffer from addiction. This is a blind spot that can grow from a person's own sheltered experiences. If society truly wishes to move toward helping those that struggle in the mainstream, supportive programs should be built through the perspective of those that have lived experience.

To understand where gaps exist, we ought to ask those that have fallen through the cracks to help guide the process. Programming and services should be developed in consultation with the individuals who have suffered rather than what society thinks the individuals need. Often, services are a blanket approach due to the sheer quantity of those requiring them. Effective treatment plans require a variety of services to suit an individual's specific needs, which can be difficult to implement due to the substantial amount of infrastructure and financial investment necessary. Still, the question should be asked as to what role individual involvement and accountability play in the process. A person-centered approach whereby the individual is engaged in identifying supports allows for something that they do not always get: A sense of control.

When the long-term effects of trauma are examined, the pervasive theme of control becomes apparent. When any person in society feels a lack of control over their own situation, they can develop a sense of frustration and anger (Raz et al., 2023). For those with a history of trauma that suffer from addiction or struggle to maintain basic human needs, there is often little in their lives they can control. At every turn they are met with roadblocks set against restoration of their own lives, which can further degrade their self-esteem, self-worth, and confidence. While it is important that basic needs such as shelter, sleep, and food are met, society should better support offenders through programs that genuinely grow their identity and self-esteem. If someone is to invest in themselves, they require meaning and purpose in their lives. Broader society should play a role in growing intrinsic self-worth by developing strategies that find the value a person provides and foster the belief in these individuals that they matter and have something to contribute.

How Trauma Surfaces in Police Officers

One subgroup within society that has developed its own code of conduct (both formal and informal) is the profession of policing. Transgressions against the rules of the profession are met with either legal sanctions or social ostracization. When this happens, the individual that stepped out of the expected behavior can suffer on two fronts: There may be a distancing of the member from their peers which can lead to feelings of abandonment and isolation.

Much like those in generalized society who are alienated and become a bystander to the rest of the population, police officers that become alienated from the profession quickly lose their identity and sense of purpose. For a profession that typically employs very progressive, motivated, and driven individuals, a loss of purpose and direction can cause immense levels of distress. Though a career in policing often draws those with a high degree of self-confidence and competence, these qualities can deteriorate if an officer begins to feel alienated or ostracized. When there is a transgression (real or perceived), there grows very quickly a confidence gap within the officer themselves, and it contributes to overwhelming self-stigmatization and a decrease in feelings of self-worth. Without effective social engagement with the officer's trusted peer group, that gap may widen as time progresses. When an individual already feels bad about themselves, the effects of trauma or organizational issues can have a greater psychological toll on the person, further affecting their well-being and resilience.

Police officer transgressions in Canada can be born out of poor decision-making or an outright decision to engage in unethical behavior. Adequate time is generally not given to dissecting which category a police officer's behavior falls into. However, when police discipline focuses solely on the premise that all actions are direct indications of bad moral character, it has the potential to further erode an officer's image of themselves. Once again, we are confronted with the dangerous thinking trap: "I did a bad thing, so I am a bad person." An ethical checkpoint that can be employed is to differentiate between "mistakes of the heart" and "mistakes of the mind." Mistakes of the heart have the right intention but fail in execution, whereas mistakes of the mind are knowing disregard of a policy, rule, or law. It is highly recommended that leaders handle these two situations differently when administering discipline.

Much like those in general society that struggle with acceptable behavior due to prior trauma or adverse childhood experiences, police officers that struggle with appropriate decision-making can be the victim of high-stress environments that are routinely exposed to trauma. Repeated exposure to such environments can change the structure of the human brain, which can lead to anger, emotional outbursts, impatience, inhibited decision-making, and difficulty in social settings (McEwen, 2000; Solomon & Heide, 2005).

Humans are social beings, generally seeking connection with those like themselves. When forming healthy connections, individuals may see a decrease in stress and anxiety simply by being in the presence of a trusted person who is, themselves, calm and emotionally regulated. Conversely, individuals can see their stress or anxiety increase if they find themselves close to someone that is experiencing the same physiological reaction (Gerbarg et al., 2019). This issue underscores the importance of organizational health and wellness, which in turn bears influence on individual officer-offender interactions.

Healthy and supported police officers with regulated systems are better able to handle stressful conflicts on the street (Bisson Desrochers et al., 2021), which can decrease poor decision-making, complaints, and negative public perceptions of the individual officer, its organization, and the profession. For example, an agitated offender with a history of trauma is high on street drugs and causing damage to property due to dysregulation. A police officer that has been exposed to repeated trauma over several years within the profession responds to assist the unregulated individual. The police officer is also suffering with a decreased level of resilience and patience due to their own history. Upon arrival, the offender's agitated state induces a reaction within the officer who is also struggling to control their own physiological response. These two humans, both bringing their own history into the equation, then erupt like mixing baking soda and vinegar: The resulting conflict was predisposed long before the two came into contact.

When considered through this lens, it can be said that offenders and police officers with operational stress or PTSD share some similarities. That said, it would be through some mutual understanding that police-offender relationships could be repaired. Despite an understanding that there is a biological reason that inhibits a person's ability to remain calm in times of stress and that much of those reactions are out of a person's control if there is a history of trauma, there are strategies to mitigate the volatile reactions that can occur when two dysregulated individuals clash.

Public Expectations of Police When Conflict Arises

There is a general belief that police officers and other public safety personnel should hold themselves to a higher standard than the public. Unfortunately, it can be difficult to meet that standard when an officer's biology is struggling to regulate in times of stress. This is an aspect of emergency service work that is rarely spoken of. Rarely among peers, in popular media or in the courts do emergency personnel speak of fear, anxiety, and the visceral reactions they have felt due to a critical event. In current policing culture and in public discourse, including media, much focus is put on the police officer's ability to de-escalate others. Such skills are important in decreasing use of force and potential for police liability and injury (Olivia et al., 2010), but emphasis should also be placed on building police officers' ability to control their own emotions. As invested as the profession is in an officer's capacity to de-escalate others, it should be equally invested in an officer's ability to not escalate themselves. It does fall to these civil servants to rise above their own situations and help those that are in the throes of crisis; however, there is much that can be done to proactively assist them. Prior to being exposed to stressful situations, public safety personnel should identify their individual triggers that can impede clear thoughts and decision-making. Knowing their triggers allows them to employ strategies, such as intentional breathing, mindfulness, etc., that encourage calmness in challenging situations.

A further means of ensuring emergency personnel are well-regulated is through physical space. When a person works 40 hours a week in an environment where their safety is always a consideration and they are exposed to repeated trauma, they can struggle to communicate with others and decipher social cues. These working conditions can lead to hypervigilance and overwhelming concern for personal space. This can translate into extremely firm verbal direction from emergency personnel to those around them during a call for service. Police officers, firefighters, and paramedics require room to conduct their work. In a situation where groups or noninvolved individuals crowd the scene of a critical incident, emergency workers can feel stifled, claustrophobic, or threatened based on others being near them. If these feelings accompany prior trauma, a visceral reaction can occur. The difficulty is that the public does not always know why space is required, and officers may not always have the time to explain, which can create conflict when officers attempt to create a safe space. Consequently, firm verbal direction or even physical movement of a person away from the scene of an event can be interpreted negatively by the public.

Additional complications arise due to the increasing trend of the public recording such instances, clips of which are often shared out of context and without consideration for the many complex factors that contribute to the circumstances and the general nature of police response. Without those details, it can be perceived that in instances where officers are managing crowds and attempting to control the scene of a critical incident, they are deliberately trying to inhibit public viewing or recording. However, what they are often trying to achieve is safety for themselves and the public without distractions or competing priorities.

We should also consider how, with the proliferation of social media in the digital age, police officers may be regularly exposed to triggers outside of their workday. The officer who was attempting to create a safe space for their colleagues and the public may have watched a video or read an article the night prior about an officer in another community who was ambushed and shot at close range. Videos and events such as this become deeply personal and can affect decision-making. There are many opportunities for officers to see and read these stories, particularly when police issues and events tend to be of significant public interest. It is well established that negative social media and news media coverage, including bystander video, of use of force and police interactions can impact public perceptions (Meither et al., 2019; Graziano, 2019), but it also impact officers' self-legitimacy and the resulting confidence they have in their own authority (Nix & Wolfe, 2017). Though it has not been studied extensively, it stands to reason that repeated exposure to such stories can create hypervigilance within frontline officers, further impacting relations with the public and perceptions of policing. It is fair to believe that a police officer can experience vicarious trauma when watching or reading about events involving other officers.

It is also worth noting that there is a preexisting incongruence between the mindset of police officers and those requesting police assistance. When a victim of crime requests police presence, they are often operating in an emotional state due to the nature of their personal situation (Pogrebin & Poole, 1991; Adams & Buck, 2010). A police officer arriving at a call will (trauma-history aside) likely bring a more logic-oriented mindset to the situation. This divergence can cause conflict. However, the consequences can become more dire when both individuals are operating in an emotional mindset due to their own histories. As such, an end goal during public-officer interactions is to have both sides move to a logical mindset as quickly as possible. This can be accomplished through direct, genuine, and open communication. When the situation is safe enough to allow for effective communication with members of the public, police officers should take the opportunity to build rapport and trust.

Building Resilience in Community Members

The great paradox of resiliency is that it can only be built through adversity. Dependent on relationships, skills, and prior experiences, some individuals may have stronger foundations than others; but fundamentally, it is exposure to adversity that defines and reinforces how resilient an individual may be. Those who live a relatively protected existence absent of significant physical, emotional, or psychological struggles may not cultivate the strategies and individual coping mechanisms required to adjust to hardship. Confidence and mindset are also central to resiliency. A person lacking in confidence may view a challenging situation as a hurdle where a confident person may view it as a passing moment in time. One mindset may disrupt the individual or cause regression, while the other may allow the individual to move forward. Confidence, like resiliency, is learned through experience and in supportive environments. Despite this, there is a fine balance between growing character and experiencing frequent, sustained adversity that may overwhelm and lead to trauma.

Adversity creates challenge, but it should not be viewed as an inhibitor to growth. Achieving the mindset necessary to perceive it as opportunity can be difficult to foster in those with trauma. A strategy for encouraging a positive shift in mindset is through relationships and healthy role modeling (Morgenroth et al., 2015). When an individual speaks with a trusted member of their community, the challenge can be reframed through empathy and understanding. Such role models can offer insight by speaking to the adversity they have faced and the strategies they have employed to overcome it. They are an example others can reference to feel empowered in their own struggles. Through such interactions and strategic questioning, a person can be guided to cast more informed opinions of themselves and their abilities, replacing the negative self-perceptions that inhibit them from overcoming challenges.

Here we see the importance of community and connection in fostering resilience. Members of the public and police officers alike should recognize that such social support and positive relationships are a prerequisite for success, particularly when it comes to growth and confidence-building that directly translates to resilience.

In Conclusion

Regardless of the individual's background—police officer or offender—exposure to trauma has adverse impacts that can greatly impede their success. An offender with underdeveloped social and communication skills and an inability to regulate their physiological response shares symptomology akin to a trauma-exposed police officer that may have similar issues with dysregulation. In recognizing these struggles, we can begin to understand why empathy and compassion are important aspects of community policing. The need to recognize an officer as more than simply a badge number, or an offender or member of the public as more than a file number, is deeply rooted in society's ability to build human-centered responses to the complex issues that many struggle with.

We also cannot underestimate the bearing that the COVID-19 pandemic has had on those challenged by and recovering from trauma. Virtually all segments of society have reckoned with the long-term psychological effects of various regulations and public safety measures. The collective capacity to weather hard times, financial difficulties, family strife, and other hardships exacerbates preexisting personal struggles. With less resilience to handle daily pressures, many in society are quicker to turn toward anger or violence. Those with a history of personal trauma or public safety personnel that are repeatedly exposed to trauma are more at risk to aggressive behaviors due to an overbearing weariness that the pandemic has introduced.

There is considerable focus on the mental health of public safety personnel such as police officers, justifiably so considering police officers are exposed to routine trauma through the course of their daily duties. This same focus is not afforded to offenders when it is evident that those committing crimes often have histories of adverse childhood experiences, trauma, abuse, and addiction. A societal shift whereby an offender is provided the opportunity to explain what happened to them as opposed to what is wrong with them may allow for meaningful criminal justice improvements. Though more can and should be done to support the mental health of emergency responders, it only goes so far when those they are interacting with do not receive proper support for their own struggles.

References

Adams, G., & Buck, J. (2010). Social stressors and strain among police officers: It's not just the bad guys. *Criminal Justice and Behavior, 37*(9), 1030–1040. https://doi.org/10.1177/0093854810374282

Baier, M. (2013). Relations between social and legal norms. In M. Baier (Ed.), *Social and legal norms: Toward a socio-legal understanding of normativity* (pp. 53–70). Routledge.

Bettache, K., Hamamura, T., Amrani Idrissi, J., Amenyogbo, R. G., & Chiu, C. (2019). Monitoring moral virtue: When the moral transgressions of in-group members are judged more severely. *Journal of Cross-Cultural Psychology, 50*(2), 268–284. https://doi.org/10.1177/0022022118814687

Bisson Desrochers, A., Rouleau, I., Angehrn, A., Vasiliadis, H. M., Saumier, D., & Brunet, A. (2021). Trauma on duty: Cognitive functioning in police officers with and without post-traumatic stress disorder (PTSD). *European Journal of Psychotraumatology, 12*(1), 1959117. https://doi.org/10.1080/20008198.2021.1959117

Gerbarg, P., Brown, R., Streeter, C., Katzman, M., & Vermani, M. (2019). Breath practices for survivor and caregiver stress, depression, and post-traumatic stress disorder: Connection, co-regulation, compassion. *OBM Integrative and Complementary Medicine, 4*(3), 1–31.

Graziano, L. M. (2019). News media and perceptions of police: A state-of-the-art-review. *Policing: An International Journal, 42*(1), 209–225. https://doi.org/10.1108/PIJPSM-11-2017-0134

Guadagno, R. E., Rempala, D. M., Murphy, S., & Okdie, B. M. (2013). What makes a video go viral? An analysis of emotional contagion and internet memes. *Computers in Human Behavior, 29*(6), 2312–2319. https://doi.org/10.1016/j.chb.2013.04.016

McEwen, B. S. (2000). Effects of adverse experiences for brain structure and function. *Biololgical Psychiatry, 48*(8), 721–731. https://doi.org/10.1016/s0006-3223(00)00964-1

McLaughlin, K. A., & Lambert, H. K. (2017). Child trauma exposure and psychopathology: Mechanisms of risk and resilience. *Current Opinion in Psychology, 14*, 29–34. https://doi.org/10.1016/j.copsyc.2016.10.004

Meither, T. D., Venger, O., & Lieberman, J. D. (2019). Police use of force and its video coverage: An experimental study of the impact of media source and content on public perceptions. *Journal of Criminal Justice, 60*, 35–46. https://doi.org/10.1016/j.jcrimjus.2018.10.006

Morgenroth, T., Ryan, M. K., & Peters, K. (2015). The motivational theory of role modeling: How role models influence role aspirants' goals. *Review of General Psychology, 19*(4), 465–483. https://doi.org/10.1037/gpr0000059

Nix, J., & Wolfe, S. E. (2017). The impact of negative publicity on police self-legitimacy. *Justice Quarterly, 34*(1), 84–108. https://doi.org/10.1080/07418825.2015.1102954

Olivia, J. R., Morgan, R., & Compton, M. T. (2010). A practical overview of De-escalation skills in law enforcement: Helping individuals in crisis while reducing police liability and injury. *Journal of Police Crisis Negotiations, 10*(1–2), 15–29. https://doi.org/10.1080/15332581003785421

Pogrebin, M. R., & Poole, E. D. (1991). Police and tragic events: The management of emotions. *Journal of Criminal Justice, 19*(4), 395–403. https://doi.org/10.1016/0047-2352(91)90036-U

Raz, A., Rubinstein, R., Shadach, E., Chaikin, G., Ben Yehuda, A., Tatsa-Laur, L., et al. (2023). Behavioral self-blame in PTSD—Etiology, risk factors, and proposed interventions. *International Journal of Environmental Research and Public Health, 20*(15), 6530. https://doi.org/10.3390/ijerph20156530

Reeves, J., & Ingraham, C. (2019). Character assassins and moral entrepreneurs. In S. A. Samoilenko, M. Icks, J. Keohane, & E. Shiraev (Eds.), *Routledge handbook of character assassination and reputation management* (pp. 366–378). Routledge.

Ren, D., Wesselmann, E. D., & Williams, K. D. (2018). Hurt people hurt people: Ostracism and aggression. *Current Opinion in Psychology, 19*, 34–38. https://doi.org/10.1016/j.copsyc.2017.03.026

Roy, A. (2001). Chiodhood trauma and hostility as an adult: Relevance to suicidal behaviour. *Psychiatry Research, 102*(1), 97–101. https://doi.org/10.1016/s0165-1781(01)00239-6

Shepherd, L., & Wild, J. (2014). Emotion regulation, physiological arousal and PTSD symptoms in trauma-exposed individuals. *Journal of Behavior Therapy and Experimental Psychiatry, 45*(3), 360–367.

Solomon, E. P., & Heide, K. M. (2005). The biology of trauma: Implications for treatment. *Journal of Interpersonal Violence*, 51–60. https://doi.org/10.1177/0886260504268119

Tajfel, H., & Turner, J. C. (1979). An integrative theory of intergroup conflict. In S. W. G. Austin (Ed.), *The social psychology of intergroup relations* (pp. 33–47). Brooks/Cole.

Wolff, N., & Shi, J. (2012). Childhood and adult trauma experiences of incarcerated persons and their relationship to adult behavioral health problems and treatment. *International Journal of Environmental Research and Public Health, 9*(5), 1908–1926. https://doi.org/10.3390/ijerph9051908

Why the Personal Resilience of Police Officers Is Vital to Building Community Trust and Confidence

Andy Rhodes

Introduction

As the cofounder of the first National Police Well Being Service supporting the 43 police forces of England and Wales, I have been privileged to work alongside academics, thought leaders, and frontline practitioners from across the world. Since its inception in 2014, Dr. Ian Hesketh and I have worked hard to play our part in this global network, and the benefits have been immense. But what have we learned and how does our new knowledge add public value in an era where trust in policing appears to be under greater pressure than ever before? A key thread will reference organizational justice theory and the importance of internal fair treatment.

A large body of research evidence exists on "organizational justice," collected from a wide range of non-policing contexts and setting. This body of research tends to show that perceptions of fairness and respect within organizations have a significant positive impact on the attitudes and work behaviors of employees. A range of benefits have been reported, including the following:
Greater commitment to the organization.
Increased job satisfaction and work performance.
Increased organizational citizenship behaviors (i.e., employees willing to "go the extra mile" to benefit the organization and the public).

A. Rhodes (✉)
OBE QPM: Service Director National Police Well Being Service,
NPCC & College of Policing England & Wales, London, UK

K. Papazoglou, K. Kamkar (eds.), *Multi-faceted Approaches to Challenges and Coping in Law Enforcement*, https://doi.org/10.1007/978-3-031-62825-2_6

Reduced counterproductive work behaviors (e.g., withdrawal of effort, theft). Notably the research on organizational justice suggests that the positive impact of fairness on employees is stronger than that of more instrumental incentives—those traditional "carrots and sticks" (such as performance management regimes, bonus payments, disciplinary action) that are used to reward good performance and increase the cost of poor behavior

In my contribution, I will put forward an argument that, based on evidence, we have:

- Been guilty of staring at the wrong information and data resulting in leaders "working hard to do the wrong thing better"
- Overlooked how the shift in policing demand over the last 20 years has brought us closer in lived experience to colleagues from the caring professions who have much to offer us as we navigate these challenging times. If we are prepared to open our minds
- Fallen behind the curve in understanding how technology, data, and people can come together to improve workforce resilience at the same time as improving service to the public

It is not all doom and gloom though. In my article, I will cite some exciting innovation and collaborations which give us hope for the future where the internal relationships we have with each other are seamlessly connected to our relationship with the public. We are, at the end of the day, simply humans living in an increasingly networked world.

Data Rich but Wisdom Poor

in God we trust … .all others must bring data (W. Edwards Deming)

There are two elements for us to consider: firstly, the sheer volume of data in the "datasphere" and our ability to decide what we *do not* pay attention to and, secondly, the data we *are not* paying attention to which, I posit, holds the key to improving workforce resilience at the same time as public trust. Policing prides itself on its often forensic attention to collecting, analyzing, and assessing information and rightly so. Information sources range from undercover operatives providing intimate street level intelligence to macro public health data directing the wisest among us toward long term preventative strategies working with other agencies.

In the announcement of the paper, IDC stated that the global datasphere had reached 33 zettabytes (ZB) of digital data in 2018 and could grow to 175 zettabytes (of data created, captured, and replicated on a yearly basis) by 2025. Source www.i-scoop.eu

I am reliably informed that one zettabyte is equivalent to a trillion gigabytes. I am not sure that helps us quantify just how much data is out there, but what is really important is how fast it is growing. In response, police services have invested in record management systems (RMS) to help them make sense of the tsunami of data which is flooding unchecked into their call centers. Unfortunately, these systems have their limitations and only recently have we seen policing start to tentatively adopt technologies which the private sector has been using for over a decade. Voice analytics, customer relationship management (CRM), and the like have changed how we interact with each other, with buyers, sellers, and many institutions, yet the police culture remains suspicious of their ability to replace humans—as if humans were infallible.

I will expand on how these new technologies hold the key to improving workforce resilience and public trust, but for now, let's consider how data overload is harming our people. I find it useful to replay in my head operational scenarios which are familiar to me such as stopping a suspicious vehicle with three people on board at 3 am or attending a domestic abuse incident where children are present. For senior leaders, it is vitally important to accept that the lived experience of frontline staff has changed beyond all recognition and one of the main differences is the availability of data stored in our systems. But have we have pursued the collection of "more data" as an end in itself rather than a means to an end?

At 3 am, an operational officer or call handler will have minutes or even seconds to make choices and decisions which could have life or death consequences. It is the nature of the job. Scrambling for time while watching out for your own safety, trying to pick up the subtle cues that signal all is not what it seems to be while hearing about 30% of what the call handler is telling you is an incredibly challenging yet familiar experience. I have not yet played in the likelihood that the officer may be one of the 20% with undiagnosed PTSD or CPTSD*, one of the 65% who is getting less than 6-h sleep a night*, or one of the 18% who have less than £150 per month spare after all outgoings*. As all these factors come into play, there is another thought process which is probably overriding every other consideration … the knowledge that, if the officer makes the wrong decision because they are unable to usefully access the relevant information under such pressure, someone at 9 am surely will. As a Chief Constable, I can verify that the first reaction to a domestic homicide is to review what we knew, when we knew it, and what we did about it. Does this feel like organizational justice to the frontline officer or call handler I wonder?

What are the consequences for good decision-making? At best the officer will make the right call but will most likely take a risk averse approach which will result in unnecessary time and resources being spent on the incident while also generating even more … data! At worst the officer may, over time, decide not to even stop the car or avoid the sort of incidents which generate such dilemmas which is where we start seeing the most concerning issues arising from the relationship between data, public safety, and trust.

The principles of organizational justice (the procedural element) play out in these scenarios day in, day out across the globe. Does it feel fair that you are placed in this position because, from your perspective, the organization has failed to help you see the wood for the trees? What are the implications for how our people then go on to treat the public?

Every year, the National Police Wellbeing Service conducts an evidence-based independent survey of the 200,000 people who work in the 43 forces of England and Wales. Our survey design is based on the principles of organizational justice and therefore provides us with unfiltered feedback in key areas such as "supervisor support"; "feeling valued by colleagues, line managers, the organization, and the public"; "life satisfaction"; "psychological detachment"; etc. Without exception, we see incredibly high levels of "pride" reported back—usually upward of 90%. The dynamics at play here cannot be ignored. If someone doesn't feel pride in their work and their values are not aligned to the purpose of their job, maybe it's not so important to provide organizational support. But when we care … really care … about our job and it's directly aligned to our values, the consequences of feeling exposed to avoidable work-based "emotional distress" are significant.

Moral injury is understood to be the strong cognitive and emotional response that can occur following events that violate a person's moral or ethical code.1 Potentially morally injurious events include a person's own or other people's acts of omission or commission or betrayal by a trusted person in a high-stakes situation.

The consequences we see playing out are twofold. Firstly people can become ill, very ill. The notion of moral injury* is proven to increase work-related stress and potential escalation into severe mental ill health. Secondly we start to see people withdrawing discretionary effort*, i.e., the actions that we can choose to take or not take. It is my view that, because we cannot easily measure discretionary effort, we are complacent about losing it and we take it for granted in many ways. But it is the lifeblood of excellent policing. Compassion under pressure, going the extra mile with a victim, and putting yourself in harms' way are all discretionary. These interactions are often emotional experiences for both victim and responder, and as such, they contribute to feelings of legitimacy, fairness, and justice on both sides of the relationship. It is the focus on human relationships which often gets overlooked in the midst of a crisis event or when we feel overwhelmed by data. A caller or victim can start to be described as a unit of demand, and a member of staff may start to feel like a unit of resource. Organizational psychology can help and is helping us to unpick these complex relational dynamics, and research, data, and employee voice provide opportunities to refocus our attention away from transactional process toward a person-centric approach to callers, victims, and our own people.

Policing Complex Need

Changes in the nature of policing demand are well documented and consistent in forces we work with from the United States, Canada, and Australia. I use the term "complex need client groups" here to describe individuals, communities, and networks where there is repeated multiagency contact to provide support for vulnerabilities linked to social determinants of inequality and poor health—problems that are not easy to solve and which, with prolonged exposure, can have an impact on the psychological health of the workforce. In this section, I will set out why the time is right for policing to look at how other professions who work with similar client groups support their people while also ensuring harmful attitudes and beliefs do not form over time.

Adopting Proven Tools and Techniques

Modern policing places staff in situations where there are few simple answers because of the complexity of social issues which are driving demand and as such requires operational officers and staff to think differently. One could argue their relationship with vulnerable people in particular is more akin to that of a therapist. Perhaps we can open our minds and look to that profession for some answers.

There are three core competencies of a therapist:

- Unconditional positive regard (UPR)
- Empathy
- Congruence

To work effectively in therapy, one has to ensure these principles aren't eroded and in particular the processes of transference and countertransference do not start to take hold.

*Transference o*ccurs when a "client" unconsciously projects feelings from past relationships, particularly from childhood, into the present. In policing terms, this may manifest itself in a victim who has had bad experiences of the police feeling defensive and unable to trust all police officers.

Countertransference happens when we start to introduce feelings and experiences from our own past into our current relationships. In policing terms, this may manifest itself in allowing negative experiences with certain people and places to affect our interactions with people who we believe relate to those events.

Unlike many other "caring" professions (and the police must strive to be a caring profession), we have no established process in place to put the brakes on these psychodynamic issues. In fact, we probably have a culture which reinforces countertransference as a "good thing" which may help us spot when something is not quite right to help us catch bad people.

So what can we do to embed some of these practices into our workforce strategy? My preferred option is to find ways of fine-tuning existing practices which our people feel comfortable accessing rather than adopt a "big bang" methodology which can often generate feelings of fear and mistrust.

Psychological Monitoring

The NPWS funds 8000 psychological risk assessments (PRA) a year for high risk roles such as Online Child Abuse Investigation Teams (OCAIT) and Road Death Investigators (RDI). This is a long established (and positively received) method of monitoring the psych health of our staff, and around 12% generally trigger a referral to clinical services. My proposition is that all police officers and some police staff should be provided with a PRA annually so that we can discharge our duty of care under the Health & Safety Act given what we now know about the mental health risks of policing. It's also an opportunity to mainstream a process which monitors our people's mental health and flags up problems early, particularly the development of negative thoughts, feelings, attitudes, beliefs, and behaviors. If everyone does it, there is less suspicion and mistrust.

It is a huge opportunity to contribute to suicide prevention, reduce mental health escalation, and spot problems early. It needs to be communicated as positive thing to do which is morally, ethically, and legally appropriate. It is evidence-based, affordable, and scalable—and we are already doing it!

Supervision Sets

Therapists and coaches are required to take part in "supervision" to support their own well-being and also to address issues such as transference and countertransference with an independent third party. Implementing something similar across policing is challenging due to the cultural perception of "supervision" and also the practicalities of finding enough practitioners. There is a fascinating initiative in one large UK force which has been working closely with gang units. In essence, they are unraveling attitudes and beliefs using supervision models—although using different terminology such as "debriefs."

Many forces already adopt group debrief models such as TRIM, and again these may not always be confined to the most severe of traumatic events—adapting them for more regular use may be an option.

The NPWS has worked with experts in the field of trauma intervention to develop a "demobilize and diffusion" training package, and we are training numerous forces currently. Albeit this process is aimed at reducing trauma related stress, it is an opportunity to regularly provide a touch point to encourage help-seeking behavior. It is free to forces and scalable.

Job Related Fitness Test (JRFT)

JRFT is currently being reviewed, and we are contributing because there is a recognition that we are missing an opportunity to embed a more holistic assessment of health within this process and/or the annual defensive tactics training. It is another chance to have a quick check-in about the attitudes and behaviors which may be starting to form (we know they form very quickly after joining) and put some interventions in place. This needs to be done supportively not as a "test" of course.

New Recruits Training Curriculum

I placed "new recruits resilience training" on the relatively new Police Covenant as a priority because I felt it needed more focus and attention. Since then, we have worked with the College of Policing and universities to raise it up the agenda, and many are doing great work. I believe this is the ideal time to introduce the above three practices as "the norm" before recruits go operational.

Technology, Data, and People

Policing has in its ranks some of the most talented and committed leaders you will find in any sector, and one of their key strengths can be the route from frontline practitioner to executive. However, for most, there is a lack of technical training in relation to technology, data, and the relationship with people internally and externally. Given the scale and pace of technology-driven change, it is perhaps no surprise then that policing has become a recipient of "off the shelf" solutions rather than an intelligent customer capable of demanding more bespoke options. I raise this from the outset because, when our leaders are provided with knowledge about the latest capabilities and also the personal skills to negotiate and influence the private sector, we will become the "chess players rather than the chess pieces."

Customer Relationship Management (CRM)

Most police forces use record management systems to record and manage data, and we are starting to see some exciting applications of CRM to sit above all our systems with the objective of establishing a "relationship" with the caller, victim, and also the workforce. When we talk about "person-centric" service, we can see how the commercial sector has advanced and policing is playing catch-up. The ability to allow a call handler or operational member of staff to rapidly see a 360-degree picture of the victim without looking across systems makes the experience more bespoke and also helps with risk management. The same goes when it is applied to the workforce. All too often, our people are viewed as a "one size fits all" as well and so the same benefits apply.

Analysis of demand into a call center identified that almost 50% of calls weren't logged into data, i.e., it was voice only, yet when we implemented voice analytics (a capability which has been routinely used for over a decade in many organizations), we started to see the full picture of failure demand, vulnerability, and non-value work. For most people, time spent on "work without purpose" is perhaps the most demoralizing aspect of their job, and our mission must be to remove as much of it as possible. CRM automates much of this non-value work, and given we saw over 40% related to victims recalling us to ask for an update, it's an obvious opportunity to apply tried and tested technology to improve how we interpret data and improve the public's experience of our service while also improving the quality of work for our own people.

Do you call Uber for an update? Or Domino's or Amazon? "But we do not make pizzas we deal with life and death issues" I hear you cry! I accept there will be limitations but surely getting updates about my shed getting broken into or a local neighborhood problem is a pretty safe option? Not everything we do is life and death. Public expectations are framed through their experiences of services which are at the forefront of CRM, and if policing doesn't catch up (where it can), we will fail to satisfy victims and build confidence.

Technology and Human Insights

But we can go further. Wearable technology is now commonplace for many people, and using data drawn from wearable tech as proxy indicators of fatigue, stress, and burnout is something we should embrace. When it comes to understanding what is really going on during those human to human interactions between police officers and the public they serve, we must open our minds to the ways in which technology and data are being used to monitor an individuals' health.

We know how much physical and mental stress police work puts on our bodies, and yet, until quite recently, we have not linked how we think and feel to how we behave and make decisions. How we behave in those split seconds is now likely to be captured on an iPhone and posted on social media within seconds. This is not to excuse purely bad or criminal behaviors committed by people who should never have been allowed to join the police—the point I am making is that technology can help us predict when the good people are starting to struggle and intervene before things escalate. We owe it to them.

Imagine a day when wearable (or even integrated) tech is linked to the command and control system so that, if your health indicators spike, the system declares you non-deployable, instructs you to pull over, and shoots you a 10-min Headspace session! Now there is a scary idea.

Summary

A decade ago, we did not have the research to describe how our minds respond to the experiences of policing but now we do. We cannot ignore what other professions do to mitigate the development of harmful attitudes and beliefs, professions which are not in the public eye like policing. I have set out several opportunities to mainstream and adapt and scale up practices which are already established and, together, could contribute to reducing the harmful behaviors which do so much damage.

I have set out how existing technologies are being used to complement the monitoring of officer well-being and which we should start to test out with enthusiasm.

By drawing on research and practice, we can combine established psychological tools and processes with the latest technology and create a "win-win" scenario providing improved mental health and resilience support for our people while also improving trust and confidence in the service.

Building Positive Partnerships as Part of Effective Health and Wellness Strategies

William D. Walsh

Introduction

When the word partner is used in a law enforcement setting, the most common visual representation is two patrol officers riding together in a patrol car. Partners are there to work together to protect and serve their community and to provide backup to one another in times of need, sometimes even in grave danger to save their partner's life. Though this type of partnership is the most common association in policing, the concept of partnership could be greatly enhanced through interdisciplinary health and wellness relationships between law enforcement agencies and experienced, educated, licensed clinicians who are culturally competent in working with first responder populations.

Law enforcement agencies have been generally characterized as bureaucracies often composed of various functional divisions and layers of supervision of all ranks (Peak et al., 2019). Some examples of divisions include patrol, traffic, detectives, K-9, crime scene investigations, communications, records, professional standards/internal affairs, and training. A position or functional area that is seemingly only present in a small number of departments is that of an agency health and wellness coordinator or a wellness division or unit.

Author Note
I have no known conflict of interest to disclose.

W. D. Walsh (✉)
Voorhees Police Department, Voorhees, NJ, USA

K. Papazoglou, K. Kamkar (eds.), *Multi-faceted Approaches to Challenges and Coping in Law Enforcement*, https://doi.org/10.1007/978-3-031-62825-2_7

Agency Health and Wellness Coordinator

If utilized effectively, a dedicated agency health and wellness coordinator, hereinafter referred to as coordinator, can assist individual employees and the organization in improving health and wellness and reducing unnecessary stressors. The ideal coordinator and program will include either an in-house police psychologist or a contracted provider who can support the agency and its employees by providing consultation, proactive programming, and responsive interventions to specific issues or incidents. Master's level licensed mental health clinicians who specialize in law enforcement populations may also be considered.

In terms of assisting employees, coordinators can scan the environment for potential issues before they develop into something more significant and serve as active listeners, advocates, and navigators to aid their personnel in finding resources that may help them through whichever challenges they are currently confronting or anticipating in the future. Coordinators should be trained in a suicide prevention methodology such as Question, Persuade, Refer (QPR) or Applied Suicide Intervention Skills Training (ASIST) to recognize warning signs of issues that may require immediate crisis intervention. The ideal coordinator will have a genuine passion for helping their peers along with advanced training in officer health and wellness concepts such as critical incident response protocols, psychological first aid, peer support, etc. Coordinators must work to maintain contemporary knowledge and a vast array of available resources for first responders. I have often metaphorically related wellness coordinators and peer support team members to air traffic controllers. Ideally, they will be good listeners, constantly scanning the radar, and able to help those in need land on the right runway, whether it be through peer support contact, scheduling critical incident response interventions, therapy, couples counseling, substance use disorder treatment, training specific to agency member needs, etc.

Logistically speaking, the coordinator should not be bogged down by bureaucratic chain of command reporting requirements and ideally should have direct access to the chief of police or agency chief executive officer for any health and wellness issues.

Paradigm Shift

A primary function for an effective coordinator lies in maintaining open lines of communication with the department's licensed mental health clinician. Law enforcement agencies are often hesitant to consult with non-law enforcement personnel for guidance on designing programs, implementing policies, or interventions for their employees.

Though accreditation consultants, attorneys, and risk managers have had a seat at the table for quite some time across all levels of police organizations, mental health professionals are in the minority of outside influencers, despite their professional status, education, and expertise. Failing to consult with mental health professionals can prove detrimental for the agency, their employees, their families, and even the community served. There are numerous areas within a law enforcement organization and within the personal lives of the organization's employees that would greatly benefit from the involvement of police psychologists and other qualified licensed mental health clinicians.

Organizational Stressors

As a consultant to the organization, a licensed mental health clinician can provide direction in terms of new programming and policies and how they could impact employees. If the appropriate framework is designed and buy-in and consent is received from agency employees, the clinician can provide feedback to organizational leadership through the coordinator on general themes leading to adverse health and wellness for the employees of the department. This open and constant dialogue between the wellness coordinator and the clinician should be standard operating procedure in working toward a culture which seeks to limit unnecessary stress in an already stressful job.

This feedback can be utilized to redesign the work environment and eliminate, reduce, or reengineer processes that are unduly cumbersome and create stress. Specific training needs can be identified and addressed as well to aid the employees in feeling more comfortable and/or confident in areas which are creating anxiety in their present form.

Proactive Approaches

Law enforcement officers are charged with initiating contacts and responding to emergency calls that either have the potential to expose them to trauma or do expose them to trauma, sometimes unexpectedly. Trauma exposure in police populations places officers at a higher risk of developing mental health disorders including anxiety, depression, substance use disorders, post-traumatic stress disorder (PTSD), compassion fatigue, and burnout (Hofer & Savell, 2021; Papazoglou & Blumberg, 2020). Kirschman et al. (2015) note panic disorder as prevalent in police officer clients treated by police psychologists. Artwohl and Christensen (2019) note that trauma exposure does not automatically result in someone developing PTSD due to factors such as their personal resilience and support systems. The authors note that it is possible for officers who experience a critical incident to develop some of the symptomology associated with PTS for a period after the exposure, but not develop the disorder. Artwohl and Christensen (2019) also note acute stress disorder as another common diagnosis for police officers exposed to trauma. Perhaps less commonly recognized is the toll trauma exposure and organizational stressors place on the physical health of police officers, including an early death (Violanti et al., 2021; Lees et al., 2019).

Wellness Visits

Individual periodic wellness visits between agency employees and the licensed mental health clinician afford every department member a partner in the provider. In my agency, each officer receives the contact information for our department psychologist, Dr. Jennifer Kelly ABPP, as part of their annual visit for anything they may wish to discuss between visits.

Wellness visits serve several vital purposes. First, they break the commonality of interactions between mental health clinicians and law enforcement personnel being exclusively for hiring and employment decisions, in the form of preemployment psychological evaluations or fitness for duty examinations, or responsive in the form of post-critical incident interventions. Though critical incident response protocols continue to remain a top priority in proactive wellness programming, a major benefit can be realized in the fact that the relationship with the provider is already established, which may enhance comfortability and security for the impacted officers and/or employees.

A well-documented issue that serves as a barrier to effective crisis intervention and mental health and wellness programming for law enforcement officers both in the United States and abroad is the stigma surrounding help-seeking behaviors prevalent within the police subculture (Soomro & Yanos, 2018; Edwards & Kotera, 2020; Lockwood et al., 2020; Ricciardelli et al., 2021; Bell et al., 2022). Wellness visits open dialogue between the employee and clinician as a matter of routine, which can normalize help-seeking behaviors and reduce any uncertainty or anxiety an officer may have about seeing a clinician for treatment. Informed consent in wellness visits provides officers with knowledge of the protections afforded in a therapeutic relationship as well since reporting requirements are based on the laws in the respective state and related licensing requirements.

An additional benefit of wellness visits lies in the ability for officers to have access to and familiarity with a licensed mental health clinician for any personal and/or professional crisis or challenge they or their family members are confronting in life without the need for the agency to automatically be involved. This connection can allow for officers to be proactive in terms of addressing their own mental health needs, or the needs of a peer, prior to the situation deteriorating to a point where agency intervention is required due to an early warning system alert, internal affairs matter, the officer being in crisis, domestic violence, substance abuse/misuse, etc.

Peer Intervention

Knowledge shared across the organization and universally utilized resources may also aid employees who are seeking help for other members of the agency. The concept of peer intervention has received increased attention globally after George Floyd. Programs like Ethical Policing is Courageous (EPIC) which originated in the New Orleans Police Department and the Active Bystandership for Law Enforcement (ABLE) Project out of Georgetown University, which has its origins in EPIC, empower officers with the skills needed to have difficult conversations and directly intervene, when necessary, with a peer. One of the three pillars of ABLE is promoting health and wellness (Georgetown University, n.d.). In my experience as a national train-the-trainer for ABLE, students share stories about peers they wished they could have assisted in their respective careers but how they had difficulty in overcoming barriers most people, not just police officers, face when contemplating intervention.

Critical Incidents and Officer-Involved Shootings

In response to critical incidents, the consultative relationship between the wellness coordinator and clinician is paramount to the healthy recovery of officers who have been exposed to traumatic critical incidents.

In addition to potentially helping the impacted officer and their support system, early intervention may also lead to collateral benefits for the organization and community served. Often partners or other fellow officers are the first to render physical aid to an officer involved in a critical incident—psychological first aid and the need for a different kind of partner will be a strong part of an agency response plan when put into play quickly in the wake of trauma exposure.

Trauma exposure is often included as a diagnostic factor for severe mental health disorders in the *Diagnostic and Statistical Manual of Mental Disorders, Fifth Edition* (DSM-5) (APA, 2013). Post-traumatic stress disorder (PTSD) includes a diagnostical criteria of "exposure to actual or threatened death" and "serious injury" (APA, 2013, p. 271). The DSM-5 also lists "repeated or extreme exposure to aversive details of the traumatic event(s)" and provides examples that include first responders and police officers explicitly (APA, 2013, p. 271). It is highly recommended that officers directly involved in the traumatic incident receive help. Depending upon the level of disturbing content they are exposed to; investigators should also be considered for interventions relating to their trauma exposure in the aftermath.

Agencies can cause harm to their employees if traumatic incidents are not handled in an appropriate and caring manner. Perceived betrayal or poor support from coworkers and/or supervisors for police officers following an exposure to trauma was found to increase the likelihood of developing PTSD (Marmar et al., 2006; Freeman Clevenger et al., 2015). This finding underscores the ethical obligations agencies and agency leaders have to care for their personnel in the wake of traumatic exposure.

Depending upon the details of the incident, the clinician may recommend a group debriefing for the impacted department members or individual debriefings for specific cases such as an officer-involved shooting or other incidents that result in investigations, media attention, or court proceedings.

Crisis intervention for police officers who have just been involved in a traumatic incident or deadly force encounter is not a universally standardized process among law enforcement agencies in the United States. Sadly, no post-critical incident intervention is standardized across the profession of policing for any experienced trauma—it is ultimately up to the individual agency to have a protocol in place and follow it when an incident occurs in their respective jurisdiction.

An entity that has been at the forefront of working toward meaningful change and standardization of police mental health intervention is the Police Psychological Services Section (PPSS) of the International Association of Chiefs of Police (IACP). Members of the PPSS are licensed psychologists who have been endorsed by at least three chiefs of police with whom the psychologist provides clinical and consultative services and who pass the vetting process (IACP, 2022). In 2018, the PPSS ratified and published Officer-Involved Shooting Guidelines for agencies to review and adopt if so inclined. Key recommendations from the guidelines can be applied to critical incidents impacting law enforcement agencies in general, but the specificity of some of the approaches for officer-involved shootings are vital. Some examples include preparation by an agency prior to an incident occurring in their respective jurisdiction by way of psychoeducational programming for employees and education on mental health resources available to employees, along with ways to access services and the confidentiality protections afforded by each program. The guidelines also recommend agencies collect emergency contact information for each employee along with any special wishes as to who they would like to contact their family or support system should they be involved in a shooting or other critical incident. The last pre-incident recommendation offered is for agencies to educate their service population and their local media on the human dynamics present in officer-involved shootings along with departmental use of force policies and investigative protocols (IACP PPSS, 2018). Messaging to internal audiences is another key to success, as internal transparency can often be neglected in the chaos following a major incident.

Psychological First Aid

Following an officer-involved shooting, the PPSS guidelines recommend officers receive any necessary medical treatment along with psychological first aid. A companion officer, preferably one who is a trained peer support team member, should be assigned to stay with the officer who was involved in the incident. The PPSS urges the same considerations be made for officers who were present but did not discharge their weapon or otherwise use deadly force. An important note is made that officers who wish to immediately discuss the incident should do so with those with whom their conversations would be considered legally privileged communications such as a licensed mental health clinician, an attorney, or, depending upon state laws, a police chaplain or peer support member. Officers should be allowed to personally contact their family members as soon as it is possible to do so to let them know their health status. It is also recommended that the officer and their family receive education from a public information officer or other agency media specialist regarding what to expect and how to avoid additional distress from social media, comments on news websites, etc. (IACP PPSS, 2018).

Artwohl and Christensen (2019) concur with the IACP PPSS (2018) in recommending immediate psychological first aid (PFA) for police officers who have just been involved in a deadly force encounter. The authors note that PFA includes ensuring the basic human needs of the officer impacted are met such as ensuring the officer can use a restroom, drink water, eat, and have some privacy and the means to communicate with family members, mental health professionals, clergy, attorney, union representatives, etc.

Artwohl and Christensen (2019) emphasize that this role would be best served by a trained peer support team member and that the assigned peer avoid conversations surrounding the details of the incident unless the peer support person has legally recognized privilege.

Individual Debriefing with a Licensed Mental Health Clinician

The IACP PPSS (2018) recommends officers who were involved in a deadly force event be administratively assigned off for at least three-days and that the officer receive three sessions with a culturally competent licensed mental health clinician and that the officer be mandated to attend at least one of the three provided sessions. The purpose of these sessions is to educate the impacted officer on common responses to critical incidents, warning signs to be mindful of, and resources for long-term care should it become needed. The guideline also recommends the officer's family members be involved in the process whether with the officer, privately, or in a separate family session depending on what best serves the need of the officer and their family.

Follow-up sessions should be made available to all officers, and they should also be educated on anniversary reactions in case they choose not to engage in long-term therapy or agency-sponsored follow-up sessions. IACP PPSS (2018) recommends group debriefing sessions be conducted after initial one-on-one sessions. The recommendation states the group can be led by a licensed mental health clinician and appropriately trained peer support personnel.

Kirschman et al. (2015) emphasize the importance of a post officer-involved shooting individual debriefing of an officer with a licensed mental health clinician to ensure the officer receives psychoeducational information about common reactions, feelings, and emotions that may present following an incident. Kirschman et al. (2015) continue that nothing should be assumed by the clinician as each officer processes their incident differently. A key point to consider is how much psychological harm an ill-informed clinician can cause with an officer if they are not culturally competent in working with that population. An example provided is a psychologist referring to the deceased suspect who attempted to shoot the officer as the victim during their post-incident session (Kirschman et al., 2015).

Artwohl and Christensen (2019) also endorse individual post-incident debriefings with a licensed mental health clinician between 48 and 72 h, but no later than one week post-incident.

Group Critical Incident Stress Debriefings

In law enforcement and first responder parlance, group debriefings are synonymous with the seven-step Critical Incident Stress Debriefing model developed and taught by the International Critical Incident Stress Foundation (ICISF). In this model, participants share details of the critical incident from their perspectives and then share the thoughts and feelings they experienced after the critical incident/trauma exposure (Mitchell, 2019; Feuer, 2021). The CISD model is widely utilized as a critical incident and crisis counseling intervention, even though the model has received a significant amount of negative attention in terms of research outcomes and efficacy. Both Mitchell (2019) and Feuer (2021) note that a Cochrane review of the effectiveness of the CISD model found that most of the studies conducted were not of high quality and showed the process did not reduce distress or lower a participant's risk of developing PTSD. Additionally, studies did not extensively review the intervention's usage among first responder populations specifically or in group formats (Feuer, 2021). According to the ICISF website (2022), individuals can be trained to facilitate both individual and group CISD sessions by attending either a 3-day in-person training or by taking a virtual course at the learner's own pace over a 30-day period—it is to be noted there are no prerequisite requirements to take the courses.

Group Psychological First Aid Sessions

Group psychological first aid is a recommended evidence-informed post-critical incident strategy that could be used after a critical incident. Group psychological first aid sessions can be facilitated by trained peer support teams with clinical oversight from a licensed provider to facilitate a voluntary discussion regarding the basic human needs of those who have just been exposed to trauma. The discussion focuses on the needs and concerns in the present for those in attendance and does not compel the reliving or recollection of details of the traumatic event in the session (Feuer, 2021; Shulz & Forbes, 2014). Examples could include common symptoms following a trauma exposure, an overview of the status of the investigation, advanced notice of what will be included in any media releases, a reminder of how critical incidents like the one that occurred are investigated, and available resources for officers and their families (Kirschman et al., 2015).

Major Life Events

The source of distress and mental illness in the lives of police department employees is not exclusive to job-related trauma exposure or organizational stress. Effective health and wellness programs account for the anxiety and distress created by everyday life events. The difference in an officer's personal life and their on-duty response to emergencies is that the officer has some level of control over incident scenes, though major life events are not always within their scope of control—this could lead to internal strain for the impacted officer.

Wellness coordinators working toward a culture of openness and trust can encourage officers to talk to someone when they are encountering adversity in their personal lives. The coordinator can work with their clinician to determine services that may best serve the needs of the officer and/or their family members for their current challenge. Consultation can also be provided on how to frame difficult conversations or questions and best support the employee. Being able to properly respond to officers who take an agency up on their assurances that it is okay to ask for help is key to effective and trusted programming. It is encouraged that agencies be fully prepared ahead of an officer coming forward by ensuring supervisors and peer support personnel are properly trained on how to respond to calls for help from employees and have a strong working knowledge of resources available to aid the employee with whatever challenges they are facing.

In addition to communicating regularly with the clinician, the coordinator should regularly communicate with personnel and supervisors at all levels of the organization, along with their families. Supervisors and peers should have access to confidentially approach the coordinator and express concerns they may have about the health and wellness of one of their coworkers or to loop in the coordinator on a major life event the officer and their family are walking through. The goal would be to proactively implement a plan to ensure the officer and their family are contacted and educated on resources available to them, including an active listener in the coordinator or assigned peer support member.

Family Wellness

An important aspect of an inclusive and effective wellness program lies in involving police families in the conversation and program offerings. The involvement of families has multiple benefits for the department employees, the family members themselves, the organization, and the community. Family wellness programs serve to educate the police employee's support system on the unique stressors and challenges of navigating a challenging and dangerous career with their loved one through the years. Our department has police family wellness nights twice a year. Our department psychologist provides information on the aforementioned areas and confidentiality, among other topics. I, in the capacity of the agency wellness coordinator, discuss our agency's various programming, their purpose, and how to access services for their loved one who is a police officer or for themselves. During the family nights, we ensure childcare is provided at the police station, healthy dinner options are provided with advanced inquiries into any dietary needs or preferences, and that the events are scheduled to reduce any burdens on those working shiftwork. Wellness programming should aim to not create additional stress in their environments.

Research

Partnering with research institutions or designing internal research mechanisms can further enhance an agency's wellness offerings. Research can also increase morale of employees due to the organization showing interest in their thoughts and needs in line with the principles highlighted by the Hawthorne experiments (Peak et al., 2019).

In our agency, research highlighted a general theme of finances being a source of stress for agency employees. To address this area, financial planners spoke at all in-service trainings on financial wellness. Financial wellness information was also included in our agency health and wellness guidebook.

An additional vital finding through our research partnership was the desire for officers to also have access to a peer support team in addition to our psychologist, employee assistance program (EAP), and police chaplains. Due to our agency size, it was also considered that officers may not be comfortable speaking with a coworker internally. Two other agencies were approached, and our peer support team was created with all three police departments partnering with our police psychologist and each other to address the need.

Conclusion

Though the main theme of this chapter has centered on the partnership between culturally competent licensed mental health clinicians and agency wellness coordinators, and by proxy the members of a department, wellness programs could include partnerships with subject matter experts from varying disciplines for the benefit of their employees. Additional examples include nutritionists, tactical strength and conditioning coaches, general physicians, physical therapists, yoga practitioners, fitness trainers, sleep specialists, and as previously mentioned researchers and financial wellness professionals.

Vetting external subject matter experts and clinicians prior to integrating them into an agency wellness program to ensure they are the right fit for both the organizational culture and that of policing in general will aid in building legitimacy and creating trust among the members of the agency and their wellness program components. Ongoing evaluation of existing programming and providers will allow for sustainability and growth to meet the needs of the organization and its employees. Employees could regularly be surveyed about existing programming, potential future additions, and their overall health and wellness. The wellness coordinator in concert with agency leadership and existing wellness providers could develop additional training or interventions based upon the identified needs or gaps in services for employees and their support system.

Wellness programming options such as automatic wellness visits, post-critical incident response protocols, family wellness seminars, and employee assistance programs would benefit from additional research in how they impact law enforcement agencies and employees.

Policing is not a profession that one can successfully retire from without backup. Backup keeps officers safe, provides overwatch, assists the officer when called for, and is reliable. An officer's partner is often their lifeline. Partners do not always ride next to the officer on every shift though the term partners can be expanded and include subject matter experts with knowledge, care, and concern for the officers on the frontline every day, showing up when other people are having their worst day and restoring peace to chaos. Partners can aid in making officers more resilient, healthier, and well proactively, in anticipation and in recognition of the dangerous, taxing, and difficult job members of a law enforcement agency perform every day. Clinicians can restore peace to the chaos law enforcement officers experience out of the traumas they witness or are directly involved in, exposure to and risk of death, and the unique stressors created by the organization and lifestyle itself.

References

American Psychiatric Association. (2013). *Diagnostic and statistical manual of mental disorders* (5th ed.). https://doi.org/10.1176/appi.books.9780890425596

Artwohl, A., & Christensen, L. (2019). *Deadly force encounters: Cops and citizens defending themselves and others* (2nd ed.). (n.p.).

Bell, S., Palmer-Conn, S., & Kealey, N. (2022; 2021). 'Swinging the lead and working the head' – An explanation as to why mental illness stigma is prevalent in policing. *Police Journal (Chichester)*, 95(1), 4–23. https://doi.org/10.1177/0032258X211049009

Edwards, A., & Kotera, Y. (2020; 2021). Mental health in the UK police force: A qualitative investigation into the stigma with mental illness. *X'e, 19*(4), 1116–1134. https://doi.org/10.1007/s11469-019-00214-x

Feuer, B. S. (2021). First responder peer support: An evidence-informed approach. *Journal of Police and Criminal Psychology, 36*(3), 365–371. https://doi.org/10.1007/s11896-020-09420-z

Freeman Clevenger, S., Miller, L., Moore, B., & Freeman, A. (Eds.). (2015). *Behind the badge: A psychological treatment handbook for law enforcement officers*. Routledge.

Georgetown University. (n.d.). *Active bystandership for law enforcement (ABLE) project*. Georgetown Law Center. Retrieved November 1, 2022, from http://www.law.georgetown.edu/cics/able/#:~:text=Prevent%20misconduct%2C,Promote%20officer%20health%20and%20wellness

Hofer, M. S., & Savell, S. M. (2021). "There was no plan in place to get us help": Strategies for improving mental health service utilization among law enforcement. *Journal of Police and Criminal Psychology, 36*(3), 543–557. https://doi.org/10.1007/s11896-021-09451-0

IACP. (2022). *Police psychological services section*. International Association of Chiefs of Police. Retrieved March 18, 2022, from https://www.theiacp.org/working-group/section/psychological-services-section

IACP PPSS Police Psychological Services Section. (2018). *Police psychological services section report: Officer-involved shooting guidelines*. International Association of Chiefs of Police. https://www.theiacp.org/sites/default/files/2019-05/Officer%20Involved%20Shooting%20Guidelines%202018.pdf

ICISF education and training. International Critical Incident Stress Foundation. (2022). Retrieved March 25, 2022, from https://icisf.org/sections/education-training/?gclid=CjwKCAjwx46TBhBhEiwArA_DjF1MDWzTrWQDQDp6J9F_Ktt6_GHtkT1VFC7Q0oukG6X_IVCQC7LjORoCsbUQAvD_BwE

Kirschman, E., Kamena, M., & Fay, J. (2015). *Counseling cops: What clinicians need to know*. Guilford Press.

Lees, T., Elliot, J. L., Gunning, S., Newton, P. J., Rai, T., & Lal, S. (2019). A systematic review of the current evidence regarding interventions for anxiety, PTSD, sleepiness and fatigue in the law enforcement workplace. *Industrial Health, 57*(6), 655–667. https://doi.org/10.2486/indhealth.2018-0088

Lockwood, A., Lizarraga, V., Kochanowski, S., & Mann, B. (2020; 2021). Stigma of mental illness: An exploration of rural law enforcement attitudes toward mental health in the heartland. *Journal of Police and Criminal Psychology, 36*(2), 204–210. https://doi.org/10.1007/s11896-020-09392-0

Marmar, C., McNaslin, S., Metzler, T., Best, S., Weiss, D., Fagan, J., Liberman, A., Pole, N., Otte, C., Yehuda, R., Mohr, D., & Neylan, T. (2006). Predictors of post-traumatic stress in police and other first responders. *Annals of New York Academy of Sciences, 1071*, 1–18.

Mitchell, R. (2019). *Why police departments should stay up to date on evidence-based practices: The harmful effects of Critical Incident Stress Debriefing (CISD)*. American Society of Evidence-Based Policing.

Papazoglou, K., & Blumberg, D. (Eds.). (2020). *POWER: Police officer wellness, ethics, and resilience*. Academic.

Peak, K. J., Gaines, L. K., & Glensor, R. W. (2019). *Managing and leading today's police: Challenges, best practices, & case studies*. Pearson.

Ricciardelli, R., Czarnuch, S. M., Kuzmochka, N., & Martin, K. (2021). 'I'm not sick!…are you?' Groupthink in police services as a barrier to collecting mental health data. *International Journal of Police Science & Management, 23*(4), 331–344. https://doi.org/10.1177/14613557211008473

Shulz, S., & Forbes, D. (2014). Psychological frst aid rapid proliferation and the search for evidence. *Disaster Health, 2*(1), 3–12.

Soomro, S., & Yanos, P. T. (2018; 2019). Predictors of mental health stigma among police officers: The role of trauma and PTSD. *Journal of Police and Criminal Psychology, 34*(2), 175–183. https://doi.org/10.1007/s11896-018-9285-x

Violanti, J. M., Gu, J. K., Charles, L. E., Fekedulegn, D., & Andrew, M. E. (2021). Dying for the job: Police mortality, 1950–2018. *Policing: An International Journal of Police Strategies & Management, 44*(6), 1168–1187. https://doi.org/10.1108/PIJPSM-06-2021-0087

Index

K. Papazoglou, K. Kamkar (eds.), *Multi-faceted Approaches to Challenges and Coping in Law Enforcement*, https://doi.org/10.1007/978-3-031-62825-2

MIX
Papier aus verantwortungsvollen Quellen
Paper from responsible sources
FSC® C105338

If you have any concerns about our products,
you can contact us on
ProductSafety@springernature.com

In case Publisher is established outside the EU,
the EU authorized representative is:
Springer Nature Customer Service Center GmbH
Europaplatz 3, 69115 Heidelberg, Germany

Printed by Libri Plureos GmbH
in Hamburg, Germany